MW00527772

Verse by Verse Commentary on

1 THESSALONIANS
AND
2 THESSALONIANS

Enduring Word Commentary Series
By David Guzik

The grass withers, the flower fades,
but the word of our God stands forever.
Isaiah 40:8

Commentary on 1-2 Thessalonians
Copyright ©2019 by David Guzik
Printed in the United States of America
or in the United Kingdom
Print Edition ISBN: 978-1-939466-19-8

Enduring Word

5662 Calle Real #184
Goleta, CA 93117

Electronic Mail: ewm@enduringword.com
Internet Home Page: www.enduringword.com

Contents

1 Thessalonians 1 - Receivers and Responders

"This letter is full of interest because it is certainly among the first of those which have been preserved for us from the pen of Paul. It was the first he wrote to European Christians, and in it the fundamental things of the Christian life are very clearly set forth." (G. Campbell Morgan)

A. Greeting and thanksgiving.

1. (1) Paul greets the Thessalonian Christians.

Paul, Silvanus, and Timothy, To the church of the Thessalonians in God the Father and the Lord Jesus Christ: Grace to you and peace from God our Father and the Lord Jesus Christ.

a. **Paul, Silvanus, and Timothy**: Paul was an amazing man and apostle of God, but he usually did not work all by himself. Whenever he could, Paul worked with a team. Here Paul mentioned the men he worked with.

i. **Silvanus** (also known as *Silas*) was a long and experienced companion of Paul. He traveled with Paul on his second missionary journey and was imprisoned and set free with Paul in the Philippian jail (Acts 16:19-30). When Paul first came to Thessalonica, Silas came with him (Acts 17:1-9). Therefore, the Thessalonians knew **Silvanus** well.

ii. **Timothy** was a resident of Lystra, a city in the province of Galatia (Acts 16:1-3). He was the son of a Greek father (Acts 16:1) and a Jewish mother named Eunice (2 Timothy 1:5). From his youth learned the Scriptures from his mother and grandmother (2 Timothy 1:5; 3:15). Timothy was a trusted companion and associate of Paul, and he accompanied Paul on many of his missionary journeys. Paul sent Timothy to the Thessalonians on a previous occasion (1 Thessalonians 3:2).

7

b. **To the church of the Thessalonians**: Paul himself founded the church in Thessalonica on his second missionary journey (Acts 17:1-9). He was only in the city a short time because he was forced out by enemies of the Gospel. Yet **the church of the Thessalonians** continued alive and active. Though Paul had to suddenly leave this young church, his deep concern for them prompted this letter.

> i. On Paul's second missionary journey, he was imprisoned in Philippi and then miraculously freed from jail - only to be kicked out of the city. Then he came to Thessalonica, the prosperous capital of the province of Macedonia (northern Greece), located on the famous Egnatian Way.

> ii. After only three weekends of prosperous ministry (Acts 17:2), he had to flee from an angry mob. He moved on to Berea - again enjoying several weeks of ministry, but soon driven out by the same Thessalonian mob.

> iii. His next stop was Athens where he preached a good sermon but had mixed results. By the time he came to Corinth, he was *in weakness, in fear and in much trembling* (1 Corinthians 2:3). At this point of the second missionary journey, it seemed that Paul was a very discouraged missionary.

> iv. While in Corinth, it is likely that Paul was greatly concerned about the churches he had just founded, and he wondered about their state. While at Corinth, Silas and Timothy came to him from Thessalonica with great news: the church there was strong. Paul became so excited that he dashed off this letter to the Thessalonians, probably his first letter to any church. He wrote it just a few months after he had first established the church in Thessalonica. After writing and sending this letter, Paul enjoyed a sustained and fruitful ministry in Corinth - and eventually returned to the Thessalonians.

> v. This letter presupposes a basic truth: Paul thought it important, (even essential) to organize these young converts into a community of mutual interest, care, and fellowship. Paul "knew better than to leave his young societies with nothing more than the vague memory of pious preaching. The local organization was, as yet, primitive, but evidently it was sufficient to maintain itself and carry on the business of the church, when the guiding hand of the missionary was removed." (Moffatt)

c. **Grace to you and peace from God our Father and the Lord Jesus Christ**: Paul brought this customary greeting to the Thessalonian Christians, hailing them in the **grace** and **peace** of God the Father.

i. Morris on **grace to you**: "The change in the Greek form though slight in sound [*chairein* to *charis*], is great in sense. It is a big step from 'greeting' to 'grace.' Grace fundamentally means 'that which causes joy,' a shade of meaning we may still discern when we speak of a graceful action or the social graces. It comes to mean 'favor,' 'kindness,' and then especially God's kindness to man in providing for his spiritual needs in Christ."

ii. Hiebert on **God our Father and the Lord Jesus Christ**: "Paul's construction, which unites the two under the government of the one preposition in (*en*), places the two names side by side on a basis of equality. It is a clear witness to his conviction concerning the deity of Jesus Christ."

iii. "It is important to notice that the first words of 1 Thessalonians are in the form usual at the beginning of a letter of this period. What follows is not a theological treatise, but a real letter arising out of the situation in which the Apostle and his friends find themselves." (Morris)

2. (2) Paul's gratitude to God.

We give thanks to God always for you all, making mention of you in our prayers,

a. **We give thanks to God always for you all**: When Paul thought of the Christians in Thessalonica, his heart filled with gratitude. Paul started the church there in less than ideal circumstances, being run out of town after only three weekends with them (Acts 17:1-10). Yet the church was strong and full of life. Paul knew that this work was beyond him and his abilities and that it was the work of God.

i. "The regularly recurring nature of the thanksgiving is also implied in the use of the present tense of the verb. It is their practice to give thanks to God 'continually, never skipping a single day.'" (Hiebert)

b. **Making mention of you in our prayers**: When Paul prayed for people and churches, it wasn't necessarily a long time of intercession. He often simply made **mention** of a church or a person in prayer (Romans 1:9, Ephesians 1:16, Philemon 1:4).

i. "And not Paul alone. The plural implies that all three missionaries prayed together." (Moffatt)

3. (3-4) Why Paul gave thanks to God for the Thessalonian Christians.

Remembering without ceasing your work of faith, labor of love, and patience of hope in our Lord Jesus Christ in the sight of our God and Father, knowing, beloved brethren, your election by God.

a. **Remembering without ceasing your work of faith**: There were things about the Christians in Thessalonica that Paul simply could not forget. He always remembered them. What he remembered about them, made him thankful.

> i. Paul's gratitude didn't come because all the Christians in Thessalonica thought so highly of him. Later, Paul used a whole chapter defending himself and his ministry against slander and false accusations.

> ii. Paul's gratitude didn't come because the Thessalonian Christians were morally impeccable. Later in the letter, Paul strongly warned them against the failings in regard to sexual impurity.

> iii. Paul's gratitude didn't come because the Thessalonian Christians were completely accurate in all their doctrine. He had to correct some of their wrong ideas in that area also.

b. **Your work of faith, labor of love, and patience of hope in our Lord Jesus Christ**: Despite the problems, Paul was so grateful to God for the Thessalonians because there was an undeniable work of the Holy Spirit and a marvelous change in their lives. The three great Christian virtues were evident among them: **faith**, **love**, and **hope**.

> i. "Here for the first time, chronologically, in Paul's writings we have this famous triad: *faith, love, hope*. But Paul's stress is not on these virtues alone, but rather upon what they produce." (Hiebert)

> - Therefore, their **faith** produced **work** – as is the nature of true faith.
> - Their **love** produced **labor**. There are two different ancient Greek words for work: *ergon* and *kopos*. *Ergon* "may be pleasant and stimulating," but *kopos* "implies toil that is strenuous and sweat-producing." (Hiebert)
> - Their **hope** produced **patience**, which is the long-suffering *endurance* needed to not only survive hard times, but to triumph through them.

c. **Knowing, beloved brethren, your election by God**: Paul reminded them that God *loved* them (**beloved**) and that He *chose* them (**election**). The two go together. When we *love* someone, we naturally *choose* them.

> i. "The phrase *beloved by God* was a phrase which the Jews applied only to supremely great men like Moses and Solomon, and to the nation

of Israel itself. Now the greatest privilege of the greatest men of God's chosen people has been extended to the humblest of the Gentiles." (Barclay)

ii. The following verses will explain *why* Paul was so confident in **knowing** their **election by God**. Paul saw definite signs that said, "These Thessalonians are God's elect." In a sermon on the following passage, Charles Spurgeon found four evidences of election:

- The Word of God coming home with power (*our gospel did not come to you in word only, but also in power*).
- The reception of God's Word with much assurance (*and in much assurance*).
- The desire to be like Jesus (*you became followers of us and of the Lord*).
- The existence of spiritual joy in spiritual service (*in much affliction, with joy of the Holy Spirit*).

B. The cause and effect of the changes in the lives of the Thessalonians.

1. (5) The **gospel** caused the changes in the Thessalonian Christians.

For our gospel did not come to you in word only, but also in power, and in the Holy Spirit and in much assurance, as you know what kind of men we were among you for your sake.

a. **For our gospel did not come to you in word only**: The **gospel** is not a matter of mere words. In modern culture there is an overflow of information or entertainment that often only amounts to mere words. Yet the Gospel is more that words, it also has **power**.

　i. **For our gospel did not come to you**: Literally, Paul wrote "**became to you** – proved to be, in its approach to you." (Alford)

b. **Also in power**: The message of Jesus Christ has **power**. It has **power** for miracles; **power** for wonderful signs from God; and best of all, it has the **power** to change minds, hearts, and lives.

　i. Thomas on **power**: "Not to be confused with *dynameis*, the plural of *dynamis*, which means 'miracles' (1 Corinthians 12:10; Galatians 3:5), the singular does not specify supernatural manifestations but neither does it exclude them."

　ii. "Some take the word *power* to mean miracles. I extend the word to apply to the spiritual power of doctrine... It is the living voice of God, inseparable from its effect, as compared with the empty and lifeless eloquence of men." (Calvin)

c. **And in the Holy Spirit**: It is a message by the **Holy Spirit**, a living Person, who works within the hearts of the hearers, to convict, to comfort, and to instruct. If the preacher only speaks, then it is a matter of **word only**, but when the **Holy Spirit** works through the Word, a great spiritual work is accomplished.

> i. We sometimes think too little about the *spiritual* operations of the Word of God. There is a spiritual work of God's Word that goes far beyond the basic educational value of learning the Bible.

d. **And in much assurance**: It is a message given in **much assurance**. This describes the preacher who really believes what he preaches. There is no substitute for that **assurance**, and if a preacher doesn't have it, he should stay out of the pulpit.

2. (6) The Thessalonians responded to the gospel by becoming followers.

And you became followers of us and of the Lord, having received the word in much affliction, with joy of the Holy Spirit,

a. **And you became followers of us and of the Lord**: The Thessalonians stopped following other things but followed after Paul and the Lord. Paul says that it was a good thing for the them to follow him, and he wasn't shy about saying "follow me" because he knew where he was going.

> i. This shows that Paul's message included an element of *personal discipleship*. There was a sense in which Paul personally led these Thessalonian Christians in their spiritual life. They could see his life and were invited to learn from his example.

> ii. Paul repeated this theme several times: *Brethren, join in following my example, and note those who so walk, as you have us for a pattern.* (Philippians 3:17) *Imitate me, just as I also imitate Christ.* (1 Corinthians 11:1)

b. **Having received the word in much affliction**: The Thessalonian Christians distinguished themselves because they **received** the Word, even **in much affliction**. The message they heard came with adversity; yet they received it, and Paul thanked God because of it.

> i. "The word for 'affliction' outside the Bible usually denotes literal pressure, and that of a severe kind. The corresponding verb, for example, was used of pressing the grapes in wine-making till they burst asunder, and so metaphorically came to mean very great trouble." (Morris)

c. **With joy of the Holy Spirit**: When the Thessalonian Christians faced the **affliction** from receiving the Word, they didn't just face it with a resigned fatalism. They faced it **with joy of the Holy Spirit.**

i. Not long before coming to Thessalonica, Paul and Silas personally experienced the principle of having the joy of the Holy Spirit even in the presence of much affliction – when they sang in the Philippian jail despite their chains and sufferings. They were examples of this same spirit to the Thessalonian Christians.

3. (7) The Thessalonians responded to the Gospel by becoming examples.

So that you became examples to all in Macedonia and Achaia who believe.

a. **So that you became examples**: First, Paul was an example to the Thessalonian Christians. Then *they* **became examples** to others. This is exactly how the work of God should happen.

b. **To all in Macedonia and Achaia**: The Christians in **Macedonia and Achaia** needed examples, and the Thessalonians supplied that need. This was true even though they had only been followers of Jesus a short time. As Christians, we always need others who will *show* us how to follow Jesus Christ, beyond the need of *hearing* about how to follow Him.

4. (8-10) The Thessalonians responded by sounding forth the Word of the Lord.

For from you the word of the Lord has sounded forth, not only in Macedonia and Achaia, but also in every place. Your faith toward God has gone out, so that we do not need to say anything. For they themselves declare concerning us what manner of entry we had to you, and how you turned to God from idols to serve the living and true God, and to wait for His Son from heaven, whom He raised from the dead, *even* Jesus who delivers us from the wrath to come.

a. **From you the word of the Lord has sounded forth**: This was part of the good example that the Thessalonian Christians provided. "**Sounded forth**" means "a loud ringing sound, as of a trumpet blast." The good work the Lord did among the Thessalonians became known all over the region, and everyone talked about the changes.

i. In a cosmopolitan trading city like Thessalonica, the good news could sound forth **in every place** to all the earth.

b. **Your faith toward God has gone out, so that we do not need to say anything**: Paul said, "You Thessalonian Christians are sounding forth the Word of the Lord so effectively that you are putting me out of business! **We do not need to say anything**!"

i. Paul pairs two ideas. The word of the Lord **sounded forth**, and their **faith toward God has gone out**. Those two aspects are essential if a church will spread the Gospel. First, they need a message to spread, and that message first needs to impact *their own* lives. Second, they need the **faith** to go out, so that their **faith toward God** goes out to all the world.

ii. "The mere *preaching* of the Gospel has done much to convince and convert sinners; but the *lives* of the sincere followers of Christ, as *illustrative* of the truth of these doctrines, have done much more." (Clarke)

iii. "Everybody asked, 'Why, what has happened to these Thessalonians? These people have broken their idols: they worship the one God; they trust in Jesus. They are no longer drunken, dishonest, impure, contentious.' Everybody talked of what had taken place among these converted people. Oh, for conversions, plentiful, clear, singular, and manifest; that so the word of God may sound out! Our converts are our best advertisements and arguments." (Spurgeon)

c. **How you turned to God from idols to serve the living and true God, and to wait for His Son from heaven**: When the Thessalonians received the Word of God from Paul, they responded to it by leaving their **idols**, and they gave themselves to **serve the living and true God**. Their reception of the Word and their faith in God was shown as true because they *did* something with the Word of God.

i. **To serve the living and true God**: It seems that the verb *douleuo* (**to serve**) was apparently never used in a religious sense in pagan literature. Hiebert quotes Denney: "No Greek or Roman could take in the idea of 'serving' a God... There was no room for it in his religion; his conception of the gods did not admit of it. If life was to be a moral service rendered to God, it must be to a God quite different from any to whom he was introduced by his ancestral worship."

ii. **To wait for His Son from heaven**: "Oh! This is a high mark of grace, when the Christian expects his Lord to come, and lives like one that expects him every moment. If you and I knew to-night that the Lord would come before this service was over, in what state of heart should we sit in these pews? In that state of heart we ought to be." (Spurgeon)

d. **Even Jesus who delivers us from the wrath to come**: Paul pointed to the essence of salvation in saying Jesus **delivers us from the wrath to come**. We are saved **from** something, and that something is the righteous **wrath** of a holy God.

i. Later in this letter, Paul used the expression *God did not appoint us to wrath* (1 Thessalonians 5:9) to refer to God's deliverance of His people in the context of the wrath to come upon the world in the last days. He may have the same idea in mind here. "Used technically, as it so frequently is in the NT, 'wrath' (*orges*) is a title for the period just before Messiah's kingdom on earth, when God will afflict earth's inhabitants with an unparalleled series of physical torments because of their rejection of His will." (Thomas)

ii. Whether he means the wrath of the Great Tribulation or the ultimate wrath of eternity, either must be urgently avoided. "A timorous man can fancy vast and terrible fears; fire, sword, racks, scalding lead, boiling pitch, running bell-metal. Yet all this is but as a painted fire to the wrath to come, that eternity of extremity, which graceless persons shall never be able to avoid or to abide." (Trapp)

1 Thessalonians 2 - Marks of Paul's Ministry

A. Paul proves he was sincere and not a charlatan.

1. (1-2) The integrity of Paul's ministry in Thessalonica.

For you yourselves know, brethren, that our coming to you was not in vain. But even after we had suffered before and were spitefully treated at Philippi, as you know, we were bold in our God to speak to you the gospel of God in much conflict.

a. **For you yourselves know**: This begins a section where Paul defended his own character and ministry before the Thessalonians. This wasn't because Paul was insecure about his ministry, but because he had many enemies in Thessalonica (Acts 17:5-6 and 17:13) who discredited him in his absence, especially because of his hurried departure from Thessalonica. Paul's enemies said he left town quickly because he was a self-serving coward.

i. "This self-revelation is not being made because the Thessalonian believers themselves were suspicious or doubtful about the missionaries. Paul is answering the insidious attacks being made by scandalmongers outside the church because of their hatred for him." (Hiebert)

ii. Paul wrote here in a personal manner, but this really wasn't a personal issue for Paul. He knew that it mattered for the sake of the Gospel. If Paul was discredited, then the Gospel message itself would be discredited.

iii. "Paul's emphatic calling of the Thessalonians to witness did two things. In the first place it showed his confidence in them. He had no fear they would succumb to the propaganda being put before them. In the second place it demonstrated that all the facts required for his vindication were facts of common knowledge." (Morris)

iv. Barclay saw the following false charges against Paul, evident from the way Paul explained himself in this chapter:

- "Paul has a police record and is therefore untrustworthy" (1 Thessalonians 2:2, *suffered before* referring to his imprisonment in Thessalonica).

- "Paul is delusional" (1 Thessalonians 2:3, *error*).

- "Paul's ministry is based on impure motives" (1 Thessalonians 2:3, *uncleanness*).

- "Paul deliberately deceives others" (1 Thessalonians 2:3, *in deceit*).

- "Paul preaches to please others, not God" (1 Thessalonians 2:4, *not as pleasing men*).

- "Paul is in the ministry as a mercenary, to get what he can out of it materially" (1 Thessalonians 2:5, 2:9, *nor a cloak for covetousness*).

- "Paul only wants personal glory" (1 Thessalonians 2:6, *nor did we seek glory from men*).

- "Paul is something of a dictator" (1 Thessalonians 2:7 *we were gentle among you*).

b. **Our coming to you was not in vain**: The word **vain** here can refer either to the *result* of the ministry, or the *character* of the ministry. Because it was evident to everyone that Paul's ministry in Thessalonica was a success, it is better to see it as a reference to the *character* of Paul's ministry. His coming was not empty or hollow, as if he were a mere salesman or marketer.

c. **Even after we had suffered before and were spitefully treated at Philippi**: Paul reminds the Thessalonians of his sufferings in the ministry. Through this, he made the point that he would not carry on in the face of beatings and conflict if he were in it only for himself. When Paul arrived in Thessalonica, the wounds on his back from Philippi were still fresh. If Paul was in it for himself, he wasn't very smart about serving his own self-interest.

i. "Acts 16:23-24 records that the suffering included a public flogging and having their feet in stocks while confined in the city's inner prison. Such a Roman flogging was no light matter; it was an experience not soon forgotten." (Hiebert)

ii. "We know that indignity and persecution weaken and indeed completely break men's minds. It was, therefore, a work of God that, although Paul had suffered various misfortunes and indignity, he appeared unaffected, and did not hesitate to launch an assault on a large and wealthy city for the purpose of leading its people captive to Christ." (Calvin)

d. **We were bold in our God to speak to you the gospel of God in much conflict**: Despite what some of Paul's accusers said, he did not only preach the Gospel when it was easy or convenient. He knew what it was like to speak boldly for the Lord even **in much conflict**.

i. **We were bold in our God to speak**: "It comes from two words meaning literally 'all speech.' It denotes the state of mind when the words flow freely, the attitude of feeling quite at home with no sense of stress or strain. This attitude includes both boldness and confidence." (Morris)

ii. "The word rendered *conflict* (*agon*) contains a metaphor drawn from the athletic games or the arena. It means the place of contest, and then the contest itself – a race, a struggle, a battle. Such a conflict always involves intense exertion and strenuous, persistent effort to overcome the determined opposition or the dangerous antagonist." (Hiebert)

2. (3-5) The integrity of Paul's message in Thessalonica.

For our exhortation *did* not *come* from error or uncleanness, nor *was it* in deceit. But as we have been approved by God to be entrusted with the gospel, even so we speak, not as pleasing men, but God who tests our hearts. For neither at any time did we use flattering words, as you know, nor a cloak for covetousness—God *is* witness.

a. **For our exhortation did not come from error or uncleanness**: The purity of Paul's message made it apparent that there was no **deceit**, **uncleanness**, or **guile** in his ministry. In the first century world Paul lived in, there were many competing religions, and many ministers of those religions were motivated by greed and gain.

i. The city of Thessalonica sat on the Egnatian Way, the famous highway that went east to west through Macedonia. Thessalonica was also an important port and a melting pot city with cultures from all over the world. There were a staggering variety of religions and religious professionals in Thessalonica. In this city, you would find the worship of the gods of the Olympian pantheon, especially Apollo, Athena, and Hercules. There were the native Greek mystery religions, celebrating Dionysis and the sex and drinking cult. The Greek intellectual and philosophical traditions were also represented. There were shrines to many Egyptian gods: Isis, Sarapis, Anubis. Also present were the Roman State cults that deified the political heroes of Rome. There were also the Jewish people and the God-fearing Gentiles.

ii. Most of these religions were missionary minded and sought to spread their faith using itinerant evangelists and preachers. Most of these missionaries were opportunists, who took everything they could from their listeners, and then moved on to find someone else to support them.

iii. "There has probably never been such a variety of religious cults and philosophic systems as in Paul's day... 'Holy men' of all creeds and countries, popular philosophers, magicians, astrologers, crack-pots, and cranks; the sincere and the spurious, the righteous and the rogue, swindlers and saints, jostled and clamoured for the attention of the believing and the skeptical." (Neil, cited in Morris)

iv. Commentators divide as to if the **uncleanness** Paul defended himself against in 1 Thessalonians 2:3 was uncleanness of spirit or uncleanness of the flesh. The *context* seems to suggest more of a uncleanness of motive or spirit, while the word itself more indicates moral and especially sexual uncleanness (it often appears in lists with the term *fornication*).

b. **As we have been approved by God**: Paul used a word here that was associated with approving someone as being fit for public service. "Just as Athenians were tested for their fitness before they were allowed to assume public office, so the missionaries were tested before they were commissioned as God's messengers." (Hiebert)

c. **Even so we speak, not as pleasing men, but God who tests our hearts**: Paul knew his Gospel wouldn't always please men, but he knew that it was pleasing to God.

i. Paul tried to make the Gospel as attractive as possible, but he never changed its central character or focus. Paul never compromised issues like man's need, God's Savior, the cross, the resurrection, and the new life.

ii. "True grace is of a most masculine, disengaged, noble nature, and remits nothing of its diligence either for fear of a frown or hope of a reward." (Trapp)

d. **For neither at any time did we use flattering words, as you know, nor a cloak for covetousness**: Paul understood that **covetousness** always has a **cloak**. It is always concealed by a noble sounding goal. But Paul did not use the **flattering words** that often are **a cloak for covetousness**.

i. Morris on **flattering words**: "We can use this English term of remarks which, though insincere, are directed to the pleasure of the person being flattered. The Greek term has rather the idea of using fair words as a means of gaining one's own ends."

ii. Thomas on **covetousness**: "*Pleonexia* is self-seeking of all types, a quest for anything that brings self-satisfaction. It grows out of complete disinterest in the rights of others – an attitude foreign to Paul and his helpers."

iii. "Where greed and ambition hold sway, innumerable corruptions follow, and the whole man turns to vanity. These are the two sources from which stems the corruption of the whole of the ministry." (Calvin)

iv. "Hear this, ye that preach the Gospel! Can ye call God to witness that in preaching it ye have no end in view by your ministry but his glory in the salvation of souls? Or do ye enter into the priesthood for a morsel of bread, or for what is ominously and impiously called a *living*, a *benefice*?... Is God witness that, in all these things, ye have no cloak of covetousness?... But wo to that man who enters into the labour for the sake of the hire! he knows not Christ; and how can he preach him?" (Clarke)

3. (6-7) Paul's gentle, humble attitude among the Thessalonians demonstrated his motives were pure.

Nor did we seek glory from men, either from you or from others, when we might have made demands as apostles of Christ. But we were gentle among you, just as a nursing *mother* cherishes her own children.

a. **Nor did we seek glory from men**: When Paul ministered among the Thessalonians, he was unconcerned for his personal glory. He didn't need fancy introductions or lavish praise. His satisfaction came from his relationship with Jesus, not from the praise of people.

i. Paul didn't **seek glory from men** because his needs for security and acceptance were met primarily in Jesus. This meant that he didn't spend his life trying to seek and earn the acceptance of man. He ministered from an understanding of his identity in Jesus.

ii. "We did not seek men's honour, high esteem, or applause; we sought them not in the inward bent of our thoughts, or the studies of our mind, not in outward course of our ministry and conversation, to form them so as to gain glory from men. Though honour and esteem was their due from men, yet they did not seek it. Honour is to follow men, men not to follow it." (Poole)

b. **When we might have made demands as apostles of Christ**: Paul was among the Thessalonians to *give* something to them, not to *take* something from them. He did not come making demands as an apostle.

c. **But we were gentle among you**: Paul was like **a nursing mother**, who only looks to *give* to her child. Though some among the Thessalonians had accused Paul of ministering out of self interest, but Paul simply asks the Christians in Thessalonica to remember the **gentle** character of his ministry **among** them.

> i. There is a valid debate as to if 1 Thessalonians 2:7 should read *gentle* or *babes*. Nevertheless, "Whichever version is preferred, however, there can be no doubt that Paul is describing his voluntary submission to them." (Calvin)

> ii. "Paul's statement of defense falls into two parts, a negative and a positive.... It is his practice first to sweep away the false, and then with the ground cleared to set forth the positive presentation of the truth." (Hiebert)

4. (8-9) Paul's self-support and hard work among the Thessalonians demonstrated that his motives were pure.

So, affectionately longing for you, we were well pleased to impart to you not only the gospel of God, but also our own lives, because you had become dear to us. For you remember, brethren, our labor and toil; for laboring night and day, that we might not be a burden to any of you, we preached to you the gospel of God.

a. **We were well pleased to impart to you not only the gospel of God, but also our own lives**: The sacrifices Paul endured for the sake of ministry to the Thessalonians were not a burden. He was **well pleased** to do it because Paul was **affectionately longing** for the Thessalonians **because** they **had become dear to** Paul and his associates.

> i. **Affectionately longing for you**: "Is from an extremely rare verb of obscure origin. Wohlenberg conjectured that it was 'a term of endearment derived from the language of the nursery.' Whatever its origin, it denotes the warm affection and tender yearning that the missionaries felt for their spiritual babes at Thessalonica." (Hiebert)

b. **But also our own lives**: Paul's preaching was effective because he gave not only the Gospel, but himself as well (**also our own lives**), and he gave because of love (**you had become dear to us**).

> i. It has been said that people don't care how much you know until they know how much you care. Paul gave both his *care* and his *knowledge* to the Thessalonians.

c. **For you remember, brethren, our labor and toil**: Paul recognized his right to be supported by those he ministered to (1 Corinthians 9:14), but voluntarily gave up that right to set himself apart from missionaries of false religions. Paul denied his rights and took a higher standard upon himself.

i. "Paul means by the phrase, *night and day*, that he started work before dawn; the usage is regular and frequent. He no doubt began so early in order to be able to devote some part of the day to preaching." (Moffatt quoting Ramsay)

ii. "There can be no doubt that there was some worthy and particular motive which induced him to refrain from claiming his rights, for in other churches he exercised the privilege accorded to him as the others had done." (Calvin)

5. (10-12) Paul's own behavior and message to the Thessalonians demonstrates the integrity of his character before God and man.

You *are* witnesses, and God *also,* how devoutly and justly and blamelessly we behaved ourselves among you who believe; as you know how we exhorted, and comforted, and charged every one of you, as a father *does* his own children, that you would walk worthy of God who calls you into His own kingdom and glory.

a. **You are witnesses, and God also, how devoutly and justly and blamelessly we behaved ourselves among you who believe**: It is impressive that Paul could freely appeal to his own life as an example. Paul didn't have to say, "Please don't look at my life. Look to Jesus." Paul wanted people to look to Jesus, but he could also tell them to look at *his* life, because the power of Jesus was real in his life.

i. As seen in 1 Thessalonians 1:6, Paul was comfortable in the idea of other Christians following his example. He repeated the same idea in passages like Philippians 3:17 and 1 Corinthians 11:1.

ii. This is a worthy goal for any Christian today; to live a life that declares **how devoutly and justly and blamelessly we behaved ourselves among** others. This is the kind of life that draws others to follow Jesus for themselves.

b. **How we exhorted, and comforted, and charged every one of you... that you would walk worthy of God**: Paul himself lived **justly and blamelessly**, but he also told the Thessalonians they should live the same way. He could tell them that they should **walk worthy of God** because his life and message were consistent.

B. More thanksgiving for the work God did in the Thessalonians.

1. (13) Paul is thankful that they welcomed the Gospel as God's message, not man's.

For this reason we also thank God without ceasing, because when you received the word of God which you heard from us, you welcomed *it* **not** *as* **the word of men, but as it is in truth, the word of God, which also effectively works in you who believe.**

a. **When you received the word of God**: Paul earnestly believed and taught others that God had spoken to man and that we have recorded this **word of God**. Paul believed in a voice that speaks to mankind with the authority of eternity, and speaks above mere human opinion. Since we do have this **word of God**, we have a true voice of authority.

i. Some people like to say that there is a **word of God**, but that we can't be sure of what He says. When we appeal to the Bible, they like to reply, "That's just your interpretation." There are certainly some places where the **word of God** is hard to precisely interpret, but there are not many such places. If we can not know what God has spoken, then He may as well not have spoken at all.

b. **You welcomed it not as the word of men, but as it is in truth, the word of God**: The Thessalonians received the **word of God** as **it is in truth**. Paul presented it **not as the word of men**, and the Thessalonians received it as **the word of God**.

i. Not everyone receives this message as **the word of God**. Yet when they do not receive it, it reflects upon *them*, not upon the message. "That you have not perceived spiritual things is true; but it is no proof that there are none to perceive. The whole case is like that of the Irishman who tried to upset evidence by non-evidence. Four witnesses saw him commit a murder. He pleaded that he was not guilty, and wished to establish his innocence by producing forty persons who did not see him do it. Of what use would that have been? So, if forty people declare that there is no power of the Holy Ghost going with the word, this only proves that the forty people do not know what others do know." (Spurgeon)

c. **Which also effectively works in you who believe**: Paul's confidence in the **word of God** wasn't a matter of wishful thinking or blind faith. He could see that it **effectively works in** those **who believe**. God's Word **works**, it doesn't only bring information or produce feelings. There is power in the **word of God** to change lives.

i. "The powerful working of God is usually expressed by this word, Ephesians 1:19; Philippians 2:13; and the working of Satan also, Ephesians 2:2. Men possessed with the devil are called *energumeni*. And where the word is believed and received as the word of God, there it hat this energy, or worketh effectually, so as to promote love, repentance, self-denial, mortification, comfort, and peace." (Poole)

2. (14-16) The Thessalonians welcomed suffering when they welcomed the Word, yet they stood steadfast.

For you, brethren, became imitators of the churches of God which are in Judea in Christ Jesus. For you also suffered the same things from your own countrymen, just as they *did* from the Judeans, who killed both the Lord Jesus and their own prophets, and have persecuted us; and they do not please God and are contrary to all men, forbidding us to speak to the Gentiles that they may be saved, so as always to fill up *the measure of* their sins; but wrath has come upon them to the uttermost.

a. **For you also suffered the same things**: When the Thessalonians responded to the Gospel, they became the targets of persecution. As they did, they were not alone, because those among **the churches of God** have often suffered persecution. The Thessalonian Christians became **imitators** of those who had suffered before them.

i. The Thessalonians willingly **suffered the same things** because they were convinced that Paul brought them not the word of man, but the Word of God. The word of man isn't worth suffering for, but a true message from God is worth it.

ii. **Churches** is the ancient Greek word *ekklesia*; it was not a specifically religious word. Christians passed over many Greek words that were commonly used for religious brotherhoods. "The force of this is that Christianity is not just another religion. It is not to be named with any of the words proper to religions in general [of that day]." (Morris)

b. **Who killed both the Lord Jesus and their own prophets, and have persecuted us**: Paul comforted these suffering Christians with the assurance that they were not the first to suffer this way. **The Lord Jesus** faced persecution, and the Christians in **Judea** faced it first. Additionally, Paul and his associates were also **persecuted**.

i. **Who killed... the Lord Jesus**: Here Paul wrote that his own countrymen (**the Judeans**) had **killed... the Lord Jesus**. But Paul knew well that the Jews of Judea were not the *only* ones responsible for the murder of Jesus. The Romans had their full share of guilt, so *both* Jew and Gentile were guilty.

c. **And they do not please God and are contrary to all men**: Paul also comforted the Thessalonian Christians with the awareness that *they* were right, that *they* are the ones pleasing God. This was necessary assurance because they were persecuted by religious people and might wonder if these other religious people were in fact right before God in their persecuting.

d. **Forbidding us to speak to the Gentiles that they may be saved, so as always to fill up the measure of their sins**: Here Paul revealed what offended the religious persecutors of the Thessalonians so much. They were outraged that Gentiles could be saved without first becoming Jews. This exclusive attitude filled **up the measure of their sins**.

> i. "The Jews' opposition to the work of the missionaries among the Gentiles was not due to the fact that they were seeking to win Gentiles. The Jews themselves were vigorously engaged in this period of their history in actively proselyting Gentiles. Their fierce opposition was due to the fact that Christian missionaries offered salvation to Gentiles without demanding that they first become Jews." (Hiebert)

> ii. "The plural 'sins' points to the aggregate of their separate evil acts, and not to the general abstract concept of 'sin.'" (Morris)

e. **But wrath has come upon them to the uttermost**: Paul comforted the Thessalonians by assuring them that God would indeed take care of their persecutors. When Christians forget this, they often disgrace and curse themselves by returning persecution for persecution towards others.

> i. "Their crimes were great; to these their punishment is proportioned. For what end God has preserved them distinct from all the people of the earth among whom they sojourn, we cannot pretend to say; but it must unquestionably be for an object of the very highest importance. In the meantime, let the Christian world treat them with humanity and mercy." (Clarke)

> ii. "At the same time we should notice that Paul's anger is the anger of a man with his own nation, with his own people. He is very much part of them, and he sorrows for their fate." (Morris)

3. (17-20) Paul explains his absence from the Thessalonians.

But we, brethren, having been taken away from you for a short time in presence, not in heart, endeavored more eagerly to see your face with great desire. Therefore we wanted to come to you—even I, Paul, time and again—but Satan hindered us. For what is our hope, or joy, or crown of rejoicing? Is it not even you in the presence of our Lord Jesus Christ at His coming? For you are our glory and joy.

a. **Away from you for a short time in presence, not in heart, endeavored more eagerly to see your face**: Paul knew that the Thessalonians appreciated the comfort he gave, but they wondered why he didn't come and bring this comfort in person. They naturally thought that this would be much better. Yet Paul assured them that the reason was not a lack of love or desire on his part.

b. **We wanted to come to you… but Satan hindered us**: It wasn't that Paul did not *want* to visit the Thessalonians. It was that **Satan hindered** Paul and his associates. Paul assured the Thessalonians that he desired to be with them, but he was hindered by Satan, and that this happened **time and again**.

> i. The Thessalonians were mostly Gentile converts, yet when Paul mentioned **Satan** here, he gave no further explanation. This shows that in the few weeks he was there, Paul taught the Thessalonians much about Satan and spiritual warfare.

c. **Satan hindered us**: Paul, in all his apostolic ministry and authority, could still be blocked by Satan. But Paul did not just receive this Satanic hindrance in a fatalistic way. He did something about the hindrance.

> i. First, Paul understood that this was *Satanic* hindrance. He knew this was not a random circumstance, but a direct attack from Satan. Paul had the discernment to know.

> ii. Second, Paul had faith. **For a short time** means that Paul knew it would only be **a short time** until the roadblock was overcome.

> iii. Third, Paul was committed to fight against the roadblock any way he could. If he couldn't be there in person, his letter will go for him and teach and encourage them in his absence. Many scholars believe that 1 Thessalonians was Paul's earliest letter written as an apostle to a church. If this is the case, then Satan's roadblock got Paul started on writing letters to the churches. When Satan saw the great work God did through these letters, he regretted that he ever **hindered** Paul at all.

> iv. Finally, God brought the victory. Acts 20:1-5 describes Paul's eventual return to Thessalonica and to other churches in the area.

> v. "Supposing that we have ascertained that hindrances in our way really come from Satan, WHAT THEN? I have but one piece of advice, and that is, go on, hindrance or no hindrance, in the path of duty as God the Holy Ghost enables you." (Spurgeon)

d. **For what is our hope, or joy, or crown of rejoicing?** Paul assured the Thessalonians that he could never forget them because they were his glory and his **joy**. His inability to visit should never be taken as a lack of love towards the Thessalonians.

i. Perhaps Paul would say that he didn't need a crown in heaven because these precious ones were his crown of victory. Those whom we bring to Jesus and disciple are a crown of victory for us.

ii. "Every man who preaches the Gospel should carefully read *this* chapter and examine himself by it. Most preachers, on reading it conscientiously, will either give up their place to others, or purpose to do the work of the Lord more fervently for the future." (Clarke)

1 Thessalonians 3 - Appointed to Affliction

A. An appointment to affliction.

1. (1-3) Why Paul sent Timothy to the Thessalonians.

Therefore, when we could no longer endure it, we thought it good to be left in Athens alone, and sent Timothy, our brother and minister of God, and our fellow laborer in the gospel of Christ, to establish you and encourage you concerning your faith, that no one should be shaken by these afflictions; for you yourselves know that we are appointed to this.

a. **Sent Timothy… to establish you and encourage you concerning your faith**: In the previous chapter Paul explained how much he wanted to be with the Thessalonians during their time of trial (1 Thessalonians 2:17-18). However, since Paul could not be with the Thessalonians himself, he did the next best thing. He sent his trusted companion and fellow worker **Timothy** to them.

i. **We thought it good to be left in Athens alone**: For the sake of the Thessalonians, Paul was willing to **be left in Athens alone**. It cost him something to send Timothy to the Thessalonians, and he thought it was **good** to pay that cost.

ii. **Our brother and minister of God**: "*Minister* is not an official title and does not connote an ordained minister in the modern sense of the term. The word rather designates one who renders a service of some kind to another. It speaks of the servant in relationship to his work, stressing his activity of serving." (Hiebert)

iii. "Originally the word denoted the service of a table waiter, and from that it came to signify lowly service of any kind. It was often used by the early Christians to give expression to the service that they habitually were to render to both God and to man. Where a word like 'slave,' which is often used of Christians, puts the emphasis on the

29

personal relation, this word draws attention to the act of service being rendered." (Morris)

b. **To establish you and encourage you concerning your faith**: Paul wanted Timothy to do two things - to **establish and encourage** the Thessalonians. Both are necessary but *establishing* comes first. *Encouragement* can really only come after we are *established* in the right direction; otherwise, we are only *encouraged* in the wrong course.

> i. "When Paul sent Timothy to Thessalonica it was not nearly so much to inspect the Church there as it was to help it." (Barclay)

c. **That no one should be shaken by these afflictions**: As the Thessalonians were established and encouraged, they would not **be shaken by these afflictions**. Timothy's ministry would help them to endure their present hardship.

> i. The ancient Greek word translated **shaken**, came from the idea of a dog wagging its tail. "Flattered, as a dog flattereth, by moving his tail; the devil, by flattering you, with promise of more ease by a contrary course, will but do as a dirty dog, defile you with fawning." (Trapp)

> ii. Without a good understanding of the truth concerning the place of suffering in the life of the believer, we are in great danger of being **shaken** in our faith.

d. **These afflictions; for you yourselves know that we are appointed to this**: Paul wanted the Thessalonians to know that their time of present suffering was in God's control. These were afflictions they were **appointed to**. As part of the normal Christian life, believers have an appointment with affliction.

> i. Some believe that Christians shouldn't suffer affliction and that God wants to teach us *only* by His Word, and not through trial or tribulation. It is true that there is a great deal of suffering we could be spared by simply obeying God's Word, and God wants to spare us that suffering. Nevertheless, suffering was good enough to teach Jesus (Hebrews 2:10 and 5:8), therefore it is good enough to teach us. God does teach the believer perseverance, obedience, how to comfort others, and deeper fellowship with Jesus in trials.

> ii. Some believe that the only kind of affliction a Christian should experience is *persecution*. The truth is that there are two ancient Greek words used to translate the concept of suffering, and neither of them is used exclusively in regard to persecution. *Thilipsis* was used for such things as physical pain, emotional hardships, and suffering under temptation. *Pasko* was used for such things as physical sufferings

unrelated to persecution, suffering under temptation, and hardships in a general sense.

iii. Some believe that affliction means God is angry at the believer. The truth is that affliction means that God loves us enough to give the *best* when we may only desire what is *easy*. The symbol of Christianity is the cross, not a feather bed. Affliction is just part of following Jesus; therefore, Paul recognized that Christians are **appointed** to **affliction**.

iv. "Surveying the whole Christian movement, he saw suffering everywhere as the result of loyalty to the faith; and he did not conceive of it merely as something to be endured. He saw God ruling over all, and knew that this pathway of pain was a Divinely-arranged one." (Morgan)

2. (4) Affliction should never surprise the Christian.

For, in fact, we told you before when we were with you that we would suffer tribulation, just as it happened, and you know.

a. **We told you before when we were with you**: When Paul was with the Thessalonians (just a few months before writing this letter) he warned them they **would suffer tribulation**. Though he was only with them a few weeks, he taught them about the place of suffering in the Christian life.

b. **We would suffer tribulation**: In Jesus' parable of the soils (Matthew 13:1-23), He described the way that some fall away when tribulation or persecution arises because of the Word - Jesus said *when* tribulation arises, and not *if* tribulation comes. The Christian's faith will be tested. Paul knew this, and as a good pastor, he warned the Thessalonians.

3. (5) Paul's urgency in sending Timothy to the Thessalonians.

For this reason, when I could no longer endure it, I sent to know your faith, lest by some means the tempter had tempted you, and our labor might be in vain.

a. **When I could no longer endure it**: Paul could barely **endure** the thought that the faith of the Thessalonians might crumble under this season of affliction, so he sent Timothy to both check on them and to help them.

i. "Paul's subdued missionary activities at Corinth before the return of Silas and Timothy (Acts 18:5) seems to indicate that Paul was deeply depressed because of the heavy burden of suspense and uncertainty concerning the outcome of his mission at Thessalonica." (Hiebert)

b. **Lest by some means the tempter had tempted you**: Paul recognized that the tempter - that is, Satan - wanted to exploit this season of suffering.

As in the case of Job, Satan wanted to tempt the Thessalonians to give up on God.

c. **And our labor might be in vain**: If the Thessalonians did waver in their faith, Paul would consider his work among them to have been **in vain**. In the parable of the soils (Matthew 13:1-23) Jesus described the seed that withered under the heat of trials. If the Thessalonians withered, Paul's hard work as a farmer among them would have born no harvest.

> i. Paul *did* something to help prevent the Thessalonians from falling under their affliction. He sent Timothy to them, because those who are in affliction need the help of other godly people.

B. Timothy's encouraging report.

1. (6) The good news from Timothy.

But now that Timothy has come to us from you, and brought us good news of your faith and love, and that you always have good remembrance of us, greatly desiring to see us, as we also to see you—

> a. **Brought us good news of your faith and love**: When Timothy returned from his visit to the Thessalonians, he brought **good news**. The Thessalonians were doing well in **faith and love**, and Paul helped them to do even better with this letter he wrote.

> > i. Calvin on **faith and love**: "In these two words he states concisely the sum total of godliness. All who aim at this double mark are beyond the danger of error for the whole of their life."

> > ii. Morris on **good news**: "The verb he employs is the one which is usually translated 'preach the gospel.' Indeed, this is the only place in the whole of Paul's writings where it is used in any other sense than that."

> > iii. "All pastors are reminded by this of the kind of relationship which ought to exist between them and the church. When things go well with the Church, they are to count themselves happy, even though in other respects they are surrounded by much distress. On the other hand, however, if they see the building which they have constructed falling down, they are to die of grief and sorrow, even though in other respects there is good success and prosperity." (Calvin)

> b. **That you always have good remembrance of us**: Timothy also brought the good news that the Thessalonians had not believed the vicious and false rumors about Paul.

2. (7-9) The effect of the good news on Paul.

Therefore, brethren, in all our affliction and distress we were comforted concerning you by your faith. For now we live, if you stand fast in the Lord. For what thanks can we render to God for you, for all the joy with which we rejoice for your sake before our God,

a. **In all our affliction and distress we were comforted**: Paul wrote this letter from Corinth, and his coming to that city was marked by difficulty. He said of his coming to Corinth, *I was with you in weakness, in fear, and in much trembling* (1 Corinthians 2:3). Yet since Timothy came back with good news, Paul had a renewed strength and freshness of life (**for now we live**). It made Paul feel much better that the Thessalonians were doing well.

i. "Never is the servant of God so full of delight as when he sees that the Holy Spirit is visiting his hearers, making them to know the Lord, and confirming them in that heavenly knowledge. On the other hand, if God does not bless the word of his servants it is like death to them. To be preaching and to have no blessing makes them heavy of heart: the chariot-wheels are taken off, and they drag heavily along: they seem to have no power nor liberty." (Spurgeon)

b. **For what thanks can we render to God for you**: Paul's thanks and joy overflowed because he knew that they did **stand fast in the Lord**. Some find it easy to rejoice in the *material* prosperity in the life of others, but Paul honestly rejoiced in the *spiritual* prosperity of others.

3. (10) Paul's prayer for the Thessalonians.

Night and day praying exceedingly that we may see your face and perfect what is lacking in your faith?

a. **Night and day praying exceedingly**: Paul heard good news from Timothy, but it wasn't enough. He wanted to **see** the **face** of the church family in Thessalonica. Paul wanted it enough to pray **night and day... exceedingly** that God would make a way for him to see them.

i. **Exceedingly**: "There are various ways of expressing the thought of abundance, and this double compound is probably the most emphatic of all." (Morris)

b. **And perfect what is lacking in your faith**: In the midst of all this joy, Paul called attention to the fact that they were still **lacking**. Though the apostle repeatedly complimented them (1 Thessalonians 1:3, 1:7, 2:13, 2:19-20, and 3:6), he was also concerned to **perfect** (*complete*) **what is lacking in** their **faith**.

i. Paul believed that his personal presence would be a help to the Thessalonians. "Though his Epistles might avail towards it, yet his personal presence would do more. There is a peculiar blessing that attends oral preaching, more than reading." (Poole)

C. Paul's prayer for what is lacking in the Thessalonians.

1. (11) Paul prays that he may be reunited with the Thessalonians soon, because to make up what is lacking, they needed apostolic influence.

Now may our God and Father Himself, and our Lord Jesus Christ, direct our way to you.

a. **Now may our God and Father Himself**: This shows Paul begins a passage of written prayer. He told the Thessalonians what he prayed for them.

i. Hiebert points out that this is technically not a prayer. "Recognition should be given to the fact that in actual statement these verses do form a prayer addressed directly to God. They are rather a devout prayer-wish... the solemn tone of this fervent prayer-wish approaches the language of prayer and is virtually a prayer."

ii. **And our Lord Jesus Christ**: "Two persons viewed as one (cf. John 10:30) possess power to open the way to Thessalonica once again; 'our God and Father himself and our Lord Jesus' is the compound subject of a singular verb... probably an indication of the unity of the Godhead." (Thomas)

b. **Direct our way to you**: Paul was encouraged at the current state of the Thessalonians and by the fruit that Timothy's ministry had there. Yet he still prayed that God would **direct** his **way to** the Thessalonians. This shows that though Paul valued the ministry others brought to them, he believed that they still needed the authoritative instruction and encouragement only the apostles could give.

i. This being true, we also need to be under apostolic influence. Paul and the rest have graduated to glory, but their *writings* remain. God has preserved the apostles' teaching for us in the New Testament.

ii. The church is founded upon the apostles, with Christ Himself the chief cornerstone (Ephesians 2:20). The foundation of the New Jerusalem is the twelve apostles (Revelation 21:14). There was something significantly unique about the first-century apostles and prophets, and that unique ministry is preserved in the New Testament.

2. (12) To make up what is lacking, they must **increase and abound in love**.

And may the Lord make you increase and abound in love to one another and to all, just as we *do* to you,

a. **And may the Lord make you increase and abound in love**: This was not a loveless church, but they still had room to grown in love, because love is an essential mark of the Christian faith.

> i. Jesus spoke of the essential place love has as an identifying mark of the Christian: *By this all will know that you are My disciples, if you have love for one another* (John 13:35). The Apostle John also emphasized this principle: *If someone says, 'I love God,' and hates his brother, he is a liar; for he who does not love his brother whom he has seen, how can he love God whom he has not seen?* (1 John 4:20)

b. **Abound in love to one another and to all**: Paul looked for the Thessalonian Christians to show love **to one another and to all**. This love *begins* in the family of God, but it must go beyond. Jesus told us that our love is small and shallow if we only love those who love us also (Matthew 5:46-47).

c. **Just as we do to you**: Paul daringly set himself as a standard of love to be emulated. We should live such Christian lives that we could tell young Christians, "Love other people just the way that I do."

3. (13) To make up what is lacking, they needed **hearts** established in **holiness**.

So that He may establish your hearts blameless in holiness before our God and Father at the coming of our Lord Jesus Christ with all His saints.

a. **So that He may establish your hearts blameless in holiness**: Paul knew that God wanted the Thessalonians to have their **hearts** established **blameless in holiness**. The idea behind **holiness** is to be set apart *from* the world and *unto* God. The genuinely *holy* person is separated *away from* the domination of sin and self and the world, and they are separated *to* God.

b. **Your hearts blameless in holiness**: The heart must be made holy first. The devil wants us to develop a holy *exterior* while neglecting the *interior*, like whitewashed tombs, full of death (Matthew 23:27).

c. **Blameless in holiness before our God and Father at the coming of our Lord Jesus Christ**: Paul was reminded of Jesus' return, because nothing can encourage us to holiness like remembering that Jesus might come today.

> i. Paul's prayer for the Thessalonians emphasized three things that are important for every Christian today:

- First, he wanted to *be* with them, so they could benefit from his apostolic wisdom and authority.
- He wanted them to abound in love.

- He wanted them to be established in true heart-holiness.

ii. **All His saints**: "It is best to understand the 'holy ones' as all those bright beings who will make up His train be they angels or the saints who have gone before." (Morris)

1 Thessalonians 4 - Confidence in the Coming of Jesus

A. Instructions regarding sexual purity.

1. (1-2) How to walk and to please God.

Finally then, brethren, we urge and exhort in the Lord Jesus that you should abound more and more, just as you received from us how you ought to walk and to please God; for you know what commandments we gave you through the Lord Jesus.

a. **Finally then**: Paul's use of **finally** does not mean he is finished. It means he here began the closing section of the letter, with practical instruction on how God wants His people to live.

 i. "The word rendered 'finally' (*loipon*) is an adverbial accusative, 'as for the rest,' and serves to mark a transition rather than a conclusion." (Hiebert)

b. **That you should abound more and more**: Paul was thankful for the growth he saw in the Thessalonians, but still looked for them to **abound more and more** in a **walk** that would **please God**.

 i. **Abound more and more**: This means that Christian maturity is never finished on this side of eternity. No matter how far a Christian has come in love and holiness, he or she can still **abound more and more**.

c. **Just as you received from us**: What Paul wrote in the following verses was nothing new to the Thessalonians. In the few weeks he was with them, he instructed them in these basic matters of Christian morality. Paul knew it was important to instruct new believers in these things.

d. **How you ought to walk and to please God**: Paul took it for granted that the Thessalonians understood that the purpose of their **walk** – their manner of living – was **to please God** and not themselves. When the

Christian has this basic understanding, the following instruction regarding Biblical morality makes sense.

> i. "When a man is saved by the work of Christ for him it does not lie open before him as a matter for his completely free decision whether he will serve God or not. He has been bought with a price (1 Corinthians 6:20). He has become the slave of Christ." (Morris)

e. **For you know what commandments we gave you through the Lord Jesus**: These were not suggestions from the pen of Paul. These are **commandments** from **the Lord Jesus** and must be received that way.

> i. Morris on the word translated **commandments**: "It is more at home in a military environment, being a usual word for the commands given by the officer to his men (cf. its use in Acts 5:28, 16:24). It is thus a word with a ring of authority."

2. (3-6a) The command to be sexually pure.

For this is the will of God, your sanctification: that you should abstain from sexual immorality; that each of you should know how to possess his own vessel in sanctification and honor, not in passion of lust, like the Gentiles who do not know God; that no one should take advantage of and defraud his brother in this matter,

a. **For this is the will of God, your sanctification**: Paul gave these commands to a first-century Roman culture that was marked by sexual immorality. At this time in the Roman Empire, chastity and sexual purity were almost unknown virtues. Nevertheless, Christians were to take their standards of sexual morality from God and not from the culture.

> i. Paul said this was a *commandment* (1 Thessalonians 4:2). That word was a military term describing an order from an officer to a subordinate, and the order came from Jesus and not from Paul.

> ii. The ancient writer Demosthenes expressed the generally amoral view of sex in the ancient Roman Empire: "We keep prostitutes for pleasure; we keep mistresses for the day to day needs of the body; we keep wives for the faithful guardianship of our homes."

b. **The will of God, your sanctification**: Paul made it very clear what the **will** of God was for the Christian. The idea behind **sanctification** is to be *set apart,* and God wants us *set apart* from a godless culture and its sexual immorality. If our sexual behavior is no different than **the Gentiles who do not know God**, then we are not sanctified – set apart – in the way God wants us to be.

i. Those **who do not know God** do not have the spiritual resources to walk pure before the Lord; but Christians do. Therefore, Christians should live differently than those **who do not know God**.

c. **That you should abstain from sexual immorality**: We live differently than the world when we **abstain from sexual immorality**. The ancient Greek word translated **sexual immorality** (*porneia*) is a broad word, referring to any sexual relationship outside of the marriage covenant.

i. The older King James Version translates **sexual immorality** as *fornication*. "*Fornication* is used here in its comprehensive meaning to denote every kind of unlawful sexual intercourse." (Hiebert) "The word requires broad definition here as including all types of sexual sins between male and female." (Thomas)

ii. The broad nature of the word *porneia* shows that it isn't enough to just say that you have not had sexual intercourse with someone who is not your spouse. All sexual behavior outside of the marriage covenant is sin.

iii. God grants great sexual liberty in the marriage relationship (Hebrews 13:4). But Satan's not-very-subtle strategy is often to do all he can to *encourage* sex outside of marriage and to *discourage* sex in marriage.

d. **That each of you should know how to possess his own vessel in sanctification and honor**: We live differently than the world when we **possess** our body **in sanctification and in honor**. Immorality is the opposite of **honor** because it degrades and debases the self. Those who do not restrain their sexual desires act more like animals than humans, following every impulse without restraint.

i. The phrase, **that each of you should know** "Indicates that the demand being made applies to each individual member of the church. The same moral standards hold for all." (Hiebert)

ii. Some interpret this passage so that the **vessel** each one should **possess** is a wife, and that Paul here encouraged Christians to get married and express their sexuality in marriage instead of immorally. Yet it seems that instead, Paul meant to encourage each Christian to **possess** or hold his own body (**vessel**) in a way that honored God. Sexual immorality is a sin against one's own body (1 Corinthians 6:18).

e. **Not in passion of lust, like the Gentiles who do not know God**: This plainly means that the sexual conduct of the Christian should be *different* than the prevailing permissiveness of the day.

i. "The Gentiles knew gods who were the personification of their own ambitions and lusts but they did not know the true God, the God who is Himself holy and wills the sanctification of His followers." (Hiebert)

f. **That no one should take advantage of and defraud his brother in this matter**: When we are sexually immoral, we **take advantage of and defraud** others and we cheat them in greater ways than we can imagine. The adulterer defrauds his mate and children. The fornicator defrauds his future mate and children, and both defraud their illicit partner.

i. "Adultery is an obvious violation of the rights of another. But promiscuity before marriage represents the robbing of the other that virginity which ought to be brought to a marriage. The future partner of such a one has been defrauded." (Morris)

ii. Repeatedly in Leviticus 18 – a chapter where God instructed Israel on the matter of sexual morality – the idea is given that one may not *uncover* the nakedness of another not their spouse. The idea is that the nakedness of an individual *belongs* to his or her spouse and no one else, and it is a violation of God's law to *give* that nakedness to anyone else, or for anyone else to *take* it.

3. (6b-8) Reasons for the command.

Because the Lord *is* the avenger of all such, as we also forewarned you and testified. For God did not call us to uncleanness, but in holiness. Therefore he who rejects *this* does not reject man, but God, who has also given us His Holy Spirit.

a. **Because the Lord is the avenger of all such**: This is the first of four reasons for sexual purity. We can trust that God will punish sexual immorality, and that no one gets away with this sin – even if it is undiscovered.

b. **For God did not call us to uncleanness, but in holiness**: This is the second reason why Christians should be sexually pure - because of our **call**. That **call** is not to **uncleanness**, but to **holiness**; therefore, sexual immorality is simply inconsistent with who we are in Jesus Christ.

i. Paul developed this same line of thought in 1 Corinthians 6:9-11 and 6:15-20, concluding with the idea that we should *glorify God in your body and in your spirit, which are God's*.

c. **Therefore he who rejects this does not reject man, but God**: The third reason for sexual purity is because to reject God's call to sexual purity is not rejecting man, but God Himself. Despite the petty ways many rationalize sexual immorality, we still **reject** God when we sin in this way.

i. Paul's strong command here did not seem to come because the Thessalonians were deep in sin. No specific sin is mentioned; it seems that this was meant to *prevent* sin rather than to *rebuke* sin, in light of the prevailing low standards in their society and because of the seductive strength of sexual immorality.

d. **Who has also given us His Holy Spirit**: This is the fourth of four reasons for sexual purity given in this passage. We have been given the Holy Spirit, who *empowers* the willing, trusting Christian to overcome sexual sin. By His Spirit, God has given us the resources for victory; we are responsible to use those resources.

B. Living the quiet life before God.

1. (9-10) We should live a life of increasing love.

But concerning brotherly love you have no need that I should write to you, for you yourselves are taught by God to love one another; and indeed you do so toward all the brethren who are in all Macedonia. But we urge you, brethren, that you increase more and more;

a. **But concerning brotherly love you had no need that I should write to you**: These principles are so basic that Paul knew they were obvious to the Thessalonian Christians. The Thessalonians were **taught by God** about the importance of love, yet we must all be reminded.

b. **And indeed you do so toward all the brethren who are in Macedonia**: It wasn't that the Thessalonians were without love; their love **toward all the brethren** was well known, but they had to **increase more and more** in their love.

2. (11) We should live a life of work.

That you also aspire to lead a quiet life, to mind your own business, and to work with your own hands, as we commanded you,

a. **That you also aspire to lead a quiet life**: This means that we should have an *aspiration* or *ambition* in life, and that we should **aspire to lead a quiet life**.

i. **Aspire** has the thought of ambition and is translated that way in several versions of the Bible. **Quiet** has the thought of peace, calm, rest and satisfaction.

ii. The **quiet life** contradicts the hugely successful modern attraction to entertainment and excitement. This addiction to entertainment and excitement is damaging both spiritually and culturally. We might say that excitement and entertainment are like a religion for many people today.

- This religion has a god: The self.
- This religion has priests: Celebrities.
- This religion has a prophet: Perpetual enternainment.
- This religion has scriptures: Tabloids and entertainment, news, and informational programs.
- This religion has places of worship: Amusement parks, theaters, concert halls, sports arenas; and we could say that every television and internet connection is a little chapel.

iii. The religion of excitement and entertainment seduces people into living their lives for one thing - the thrill of the moment. But these thrills are quickly over and forgotten, and all that is important is the next fun thing. This religion conditions its followers to only ask one question: "Is it fun?" It never wants us to ask more important questions such as, "Is it true?" "Is it right?" "Is it good?" "Is it godly?"

iv. We need to live the **quiet life** so that we can really take the time and give the attention to listen to God. When we live the **quiet life**, we can listen to God and get to know Him better.

b. **To mind your own business**: This means that the Christian must focus on his or her own life and matters, instead of meddling in the lives of others. "**Mind your own business**" is a Biblical idea.

i. "There is a great difference between the Christian duty of putting the interests of others first and the busybody's compulsive itch to put other people right." (Bruce)

ii. "Paul, however, does not mean that every individual is to mind his own business in such a way that all are to live apart from one another and have no concern for others, but simply wants to correct the idle triviality which makes men open disturbers of the peace, when they ought to lead a quiet life at home." (Clarke)

c. **Work with your own hands**: We must recognize the dignity and honor of **work**. Work is God's plan for the progress of society and the church. We fall into Satan' snare when we expect things to always come easily, or regard God's blessing as an opportunity for laziness.

i. Manual labor was despised by ancient Greek culture. They thought that the better a man was, the less he should work. In contrast, God gave us a carpenter King, fisherman apostles, and tent-making missionaries.

ii. "There is nothing more disgraceful than an idle good-for-nothing who is of no use either to himself or to others, and seems to have been born merely to eat and drink." (Clarke)

3. (12) We should live a life that is an example, lacking nothing.

That you may walk properly toward those who are outside, and *that* **you may lack nothing.**

a. **That you may walk properly toward those who are outside**: When we combine the love of our brothers with work, we **walk properly**. People who are not yet Christians (**those who are outside**) will see our example and be influenced to become followers of Jesus.

i. Hiebert on **properly**: "Means, 'in good form, decorously, in an honorable manner, so as to cause no offense.' Believers can never be indifferent to the impact produced by their example."

b. **And that you may lack nothing**: Paul completes the thought he began in 1 Thessalonians 3:10 (*that we may see your face and perfect what is lacking in your faith*). If they followed his teaching and example, they would **lack nothing** and come to the place of genuine Christian maturity.

C. Concerning Christians who have died.

1. (13) The believing dead are thought of as being "asleep."

But I do not want you to be ignorant, brethren, concerning those who have fallen asleep, lest you sorrow as others who have no hope.

a. **But I do not want you to be ignorant, brethren, concerning those who have fallen asleep**: In the few weeks Paul was with the Thessalonians, he emphasized the soon return of Jesus, and the Thessalonians believed it earnestly. This was part of the reason that they were the kind of church Paul complimented so highly. Yet after Paul left, they wondered about those Christians who died *before* Jesus came back. They were troubled by the idea that these Christians might miss out on that great future event and that they might miss the victory and blessing of Jesus' coming.

i. It is with some interest we note that four times in his letters, Paul asked Christians to *not* be **ignorant** about something:

- Don't be ignorant about God's plan for Israel (Romans 11:25).
- Don't be ignorant about spiritual gifts (1 Corinthians 12:1).
- Don't be ignorant about suffering and trials in the Christian life (2 Corinthians 1:8).
- Don't be ignorant about the rapture and the second coming of Jesus (1 Thessalonians 4:13).

ii. Remarkably, these are areas where ignorance is still common in the Christian world.

b. **Who have fallen asleep**: *Sleep* was a common way to express death in the ancient world, but among pagans, it was almost always seen as an *eternal* sleep.

> i. Ancient writings are full of this pessimism regarding death:
>
> - "Of a man once dead there is no resurrection." (Aeschylus)
> - "Hopes are among the living, the dead are without hope." (Theocritus)
> - "Suns may set and rise again but we, when once our brief light goes down, must sleep an endless night." (Catullus)
>
> ii. Christians called death *sleep*, but they emphasized the idea of *rest*. Early Christians began to call their burial places "cemeteries," which means, "dormitories" or "sleeping places." Yet the Bible never describes the death of the unbeliever as *sleep*, for there is no rest, peace, or comfort for them in death.
>
> iii. Though Paul, using idioms common in his day, referred to death as *sleep*, it does not prove the erroneous idea of *soul sleep*, that the present dead in Christ are in a state of suspended animation, waiting for a resurrection to consciousness. "Since to depart from this world in death to 'be with Christ' is described by Paul as 'very far better' (Philippians 1:23) than the present state of blessed communion with the Lord and blessed activity in His service, it is evident that 'sleep' as applied to believers cannot be intended to teach that the soul is unconscious." (Hiebert)

c. **Lest you sorrow as others who have no hope**: For the Christian death is dead, and leaving this body is like laying down for a nap and waking in glory. It is *moving*, not *dying*. For these reasons, Christians should not **sorrow as others who have no hope** when their loved ones in Jesus die.

> i. As Christians, we may mourn the death of other Christians; but not **as others who have no hope**. Our sorrow is like the sadness of seeing someone off on a long trip, knowing you will see them again, but not for a long time.

2. (14) There is full assurance that Christians who have died yet live.

For if we believe that Jesus died and rose again, even so God will bring with Him those who sleep in Jesus.

a. **If we believe that Jesus died and rose again, even so God will bring with Him those who sleep**: We have more than a wishful hope of resurrection. In the resurrection of Jesus, we have an amazing example of it and a promise of our own.

i. For the Thessalonian Christians, their troubled minds were answered by the statement **"God will bring with Him those who sleep in Jesus**." "It is best to understand the words to mean that Jesus will bring the faithful departed with Him when He comes back. Their death does not mean that they will miss their share in the Parousia." (Morris)

b. **Jesus died**: When Paul wrote about the death of believers, he called it **sleep**. But in his description of Jesus' death, he did not soften it by calling it **sleep**, because there was nothing soft or peaceful about His death.

i. "He endured the worst that death can possibly be... It is because there was no softening of the horror of death for Him that there is no horror of death for His people. For them it is but sleep." (Morris)

c. **We believe that Jesus died and rose again**: This was the confident belief of the Apostle Paul and the early Christians. We will certainly live, because Jesus lives and our union with Him is stronger than death. This is why we do not sorrow as those who have no hope and why we have more than a wishful hope.

i. When a sinner dies, we mourn for them. When a believer dies, we only mourn for ourselves, because they are with the Lord.

ii. In the ruins of ancient Rome, you can see the magnificent tombs of pagans, with gloomy inscriptions on them. One of them reads:

I WAS NOT
I BECAME
I AM NOT
I CARE NOT

Or one can visit the murky catacombs and read glorious inscriptions. One of the most common Christian epitaphs from the catacombs was IN PEACE, quoting Psalm 4:8: *I will both lie down in peace and sleep; for You alone, O LORD, make me dwell in safety.* We should look at death the same way those early Christians did.

iii. Sadly, not all Christians are at this place of confidence and peace. Even Christians have, in unbelief, had the same fear and hopelessness about death. The author once read an inscription reflecting this un-Christian despair on an Irish tombstone in a Christian cemetery on the Hill of Slane, outside of Dublin:

O cruel Death you well may boast
Of all Tyrants thou art the most
As you all mortals can control
The Lord have mercy on my soul (1782)

3. (15-16) Those asleep in Jesus are not at a disadvantage.

For this we say to you by the word of the Lord, that we who are alive *and* remain until the coming of the Lord will by no means precede those who are asleep. For the Lord Himself will descend from heaven with a shout, with the voice of an archangel, and with the trumpet of God. And the dead in Christ will rise first.

a. **By the word of the Lord**: Paul emphasized that this was an authoritative command, though we do not know whether Paul received it by direct revelation or if it was an unrecorded saying of Jesus. One way or another, this came from Jesus and did not originate with Paul.

i. "In no place does the apostle speak more confidently and positively of his *inspiration* than here; and we should prepare ourselves to receive some momentous and interesting truth." (Clarke)

b. **We who are alive and remain until the coming of the Lord will by no means precede those who are asleep**: Paul wanted the Thessalonians to know that **those who are asleep** - Christians who have died before Jesus returns - **will by no means** be at a disadvantage. Those who are **alive and remain until the coming of the Lord will by no means precede them**. God will allow **those who are asleep** to share in the glory of **the coming of the Lord**.

i. "The living will have no advantage over those fallen asleep; they will not meet the returning Christ ahead of the dead, nor will they have any precedence in the blessedness at His coming." (Hiebert)

ii. **We who are alive** means that Paul himself shared in this expectancy. It wasn't because Paul had an erroneous promise of the return of Jesus in his lifetime. "More feasible is the solution that sees Paul setting an example of expectancy for the church of all ages. Proper Christian anticipation includes the imminent return of Christ." (Thomas)

c. **For the Lord Himself will descend from heaven with a shout**: When Jesus comes, He will come *personally*. **The Lord Himself will descend** and come **with a shout**. The ancient Greek word for **shout** here is the same word used for the commands that a ship captain makes to his rowers, or a commander speaking to his soldiers. "Always there is the ring of authority and the note of urgency." (Morris)

i. Apparently, there will be some audible signal that prompts this remarkable event. It may be that all three descriptions (**shout, voice,** and **trumpet**) refer to the same sound; or there may be three distinct sounds. The rapture will not be silent or secret, though the vast majority of people may not understand the sound or its meaning.

ii. When Paul heard the heavenly voice on the road to Damascus (Acts 9:7; 22:9), his companions heard the sound of a voice, but they did not hear articulate words. They heard a sound but did not understand its meaning. It may well be that the shout/voice/trumpet sound that accompanies the rapture will have the same effect. The entire world may hear this heavenly sound but have no idea what its meaning is.

d. **With the voice of an archangel**: This doesn't mean that the **Lord Himself** is an **archangel**. The only one described as an **archangel** in the Bible is Michael (Jude 1:9). Paul means that when Jesus comes, He will come in the company of prominent angels.

   i. **With the voice of an archangel** means that Paul clearly did not designate a *specific* **archangel**. "It is even possible that he does not mean that an archangel will actually say something, but simply that the voice that will be uttered will be a very great voice, an archangel type of voice." (Morris)

e. **With the trumpet of God**: Believers are gathered **with the trumpet of God**. In the Old Testament, trumpets sounded the alarm for war and threw the enemy into a panic, in the sense of the seven trumpets described in Numbers 10:9 and Revelation 8 and 9. Trumpets also sounded an assembly of God's people, as in Leviticus 23:24 and Numbers 10:2. Here, **the trumpet of God** gathers together God's people.

   i. "It was by the *sound of the trumpet* that the solemn assemblies, under the law, were convoked; and to such convocations there appears to be here an allusion." (Clarke)

   ii. There are three other associations of trumpets and end-times events. One is the *last trump* of 1 Corinthians 15:52, which seems clearly to be connected with this same trumpet of 1 Thessalonians 4. The others are the seven trumpets which culminate at Revelation 11:15, and the trumpet gathering the elect of Israel at the end of the age in Matthew 24:31.

   iii. Hiebert compares this trumpet of 1 Thessalonians 4 and the seventh trumpet of Revelation 11:15: "The subjects are different: here it is the church; there a wicked world. The results are different: here it is the glorious catching up of the church to be with the Lord; there it is further judgment upon a godless world. Here 'the last trump' signals the close of the life the church on earth; there the 'seventh' trumpet marks a climax in a progressive series of apocalyptic judgments upon the living on earth."

iv. As to the trumpet of 1 Thessalonians 4 and the one mentioned in Matthew 24:31, we can also observe:

- The *subjects* are different: Matthew refers to Jewish believers during the great tribulation; Thessalonians refers to the church.

- The *circumstances* are different: Matthew refers to a gathering of the elect scattered over the earth, with no mention of resurrection; Thessalonians refers to the raising of the believing dead.

- The *results* are different: Matthew refers to living believers gathered from all over the earth at the command of their Lord who has returned to earth in open glory; Thessalonians refers to the uniting of the raised dead with the living believers to meet the Lord in the air.

f. **And the dead in Christ will rise first**: Paul's point to the Thessalonians is clear. The prior dead in Christ will not be left out of either the resurrection or the return of Jesus. In fact, they will experience it **first**.

i. "It is only after the faithful departed have taken their place with the Lord that the saints on earth are caught up to be with Him, or more strictly, to be with them and meet Him." (Morris)

ii. "'The order of the resurrection,' he says, 'will begin with them. We therefore shall not rise without them.'" (Calvin)

g. **Will rise first**: Many wonder how **the dead in Christ** are raised **first**. Some believe that they now have temporary bodies and await this resurrection. Others believe that they are now disembodied spirits who wait for resurrection. Still others conjecture that the **dead in Christ** experience their resurrection immediately.

i. There will come a day, when in God's eternal plan, **the dead in Christ** will receive their resurrection bodies. Yet until that day, we are confident that the dead in Christ are not in some kind of soul sleep or suspended animation. Paul made it clear that to be *absent from the body* means *to be present with the Lord*. (2 Corinthians 5:8) Either the present dead in Christ are with the Lord in a spiritual body, awaiting their final resurrection body; or, because of the nature of timeless eternity, they have received their resurrection bodies already because they live in the eternal *now*.

ii. However God will do it, we are confident that His promise is true. "Though the bones be scattered to the four winds of heaven, yet, at the call of the Lord God, they shall come together again, bone to his bone... We doubt not that God will guard the dust of the precious sons and daughters of Zion," (Spurgeon)

4. (17) Jesus comes to meet His Church.

Then we who are alive *and* remain shall be caught up together with them in the clouds to meet the Lord in the air. And thus we shall always be with the Lord.

a. **Then we who are alive and remain shall be caught up together with them**: Those alive and remaining until this coming of Jesus are **caught up** to meet Jesus in the air, together with the dead in Jesus who have already risen.

> i. The verb translated **caught up** here means to seize, or to carry off by force. "There is often the notion of a sudden swoop, and usually that of a force which cannot be resisted" (Morris). In the ancient Greek, the phrase **to meet** was used as a technical term to describe the official welcoming of honored guests.

> ii. This passage is the basis for the New Testament doctrine of the *rapture*, the catching away of believers to be with Jesus. The word *rapture* is not in the ancient Greek text, but comes from the Latin Vulgate, which translates the phrase **caught up** with *rapturus*, from which we get our English word *rapture*.

> iii. Paul's statement, under the inspiration of the Holy Spirit, is both dramatic and fantastic. He speaks of Christians flying upward, **caught up… in the clouds to meet the Lord in the air**. We wouldn't believe this unless the Bible told us it were so, not any more than we would believe that God became a baby, that He did miracles, that He died on a cross and that He lives in us.

> iv. Paul's language here is so straightforward and free from figurative speech that there is no missing his intent. "The Apostle's declarations here are made in the practical tone of strict matter of fact, and are given as literal details... Never was a place where the analogy of symbolical apocalyptic language was less applicable. Either these details must be received by us as matter of practical expectation, or we must set aside the Apostle as one divinely empowered to teach the Church." (Alford)

b. **Shall be caught up together with them in the clouds to meet the Lord in the air**: Paul's plain language leaves no doubt regarding the certainty of this event. Yet the timing of this event in the chronology of God's prophetic plan is a matter of significant debate among Christians.

> i. Many – though certainly not all – Christians believe the Bible teaches that there will be an important seven-year period of history

before the Battle of Armageddon and triumphant return of Jesus. The debate about this *catching away* centers on where it fits in with this final seven-year period, popularly known as the Great Tribulation, with reference to Matthew 24:21.

- The *pre-tribulation* rapture position believes believers are **caught up** before this final seven-year period.

- The *mid-tribulation* rapture position believes believers are **caught up** in the midst of this final seven-year period.

- The *pre-wrath* rapture position believes believers are **caught up** at some time in the second half of this final seven-year period.

- The *post-tribulation* rapture position believes believers are **caught up** at the end of this final seven-year period.

ii. The adherents of these different positions each believe their position is Biblical, and these differences of understanding should not make dividing lines of Christian fellowship. Nevertheless, this author's opinion is that the *pre-tribulation* rapture position is Biblically correct. Even other references to the return of Jesus within 1-2 Thessalonians support this understanding:

- 1 Thessalonians 1:10 shows believers waiting for the return of Jesus. The clear implication is that they had hope of His imminent return, not the expectation of an imminent great tribulation.

- 1 Thessalonians 4:13-18 assures us that those believers who died would share equally with the living in the events of the rapture and the resurrection, answering their fear that somehow the dead in Christ were at a disadvantage. But if Paul believed Christians would go through the great tribulation, he would count the dead in Christ as *more fortunate* than those living Christians who might very well have to endure the great tribulation. It would have been logical for Paul to comfort the Thessalonians with the idea that the dead in Jesus were better off because they won't have to experience the Great Tribulation.

- 2 Thessalonians 1:3-10 comforts Christians enduring hardship, promising them a coming *rest*, while their persecutors will face certain judgment. But if Paul knew that the church was destined to pass through the Great Tribulation, it would have been more appropriate for him to warn these Christians about worse trials and suffering ahead, rather than hold the promise of a coming *rest*.

c. **And thus we shall always be with the Lord**: The *manner* in which Jesus will gather us to Himself is impressive. But the main point is that whatever the state of the Christians (dead or alive) at the Lord's coming, they will always be with the Lord. This is the great reward of heaven - to be with Jesus. Death can't break our unity with Jesus or with other Christians.

i. **We shall always be with the Lord** is an important truth with many implications.

- It implies *continuation* because it assumes you are already **with the Lord**.

- It implies *hope for the dying* because in death we shall still be **with the Lord**.

- It implies *future confidence* because after death we are **with the Lord**.

- It implies *advancement* because we will one day **always** be with the Lord.

ii. "We shall be so with him as to have no sin to becloud our view of him: the understanding will be delivered from all the injury which sin has wrought in it, and we shall know him even as we are known." (Spurgeon)

5. (18) The exhortation: comfort one another.

Therefore comfort one another with these words.

a. **Therefore comfort one another**: Paul did not tell them to *take* comfort, but to *give* comfort. In the way God works, we always *receive* comfort as we *give* it.

i. "Paul does not himself seek to comfort or encourage his readers but rather bids them actively to comfort or encourage 'one another.' The present imperative places upon them the continuing duty to do so, both in private conversation and in the public services." (Hiebert)

b. **With these words**: The truth of the return of Jesus for His people, and the eternal union of Jesus and His people is to be a source of **comfort** for Christians.

i. This concluding statement of Paul only makes sense if the catching away of the previous verses actually delivers Christians from an impending danger. If the catching away only brings humanity to God for judgment, there is little comfort in these words.

ii. This was understood by Adam Clarke: "Strange saying! Comfort a man with the information that he is going to appear before the judgment-seat of God! Who can feel comfort from these words?"

1 Thessalonians 5 - Ready for the Day of the Lord

A. Teaching about readiness for Jesus' return.

1. (1-3) The suddenness of Jesus' coming.

But concerning the times and the seasons, brethren, you have no need that I should write to you. For you yourselves know perfectly that the day of the Lord so comes as a thief in the night. For when they say, "Peace and safety!" then sudden destruction comes upon them, as labor pains upon a pregnant woman. And they shall not escape.

> a. **Concerning the times and the seasons, brethren, you have no need that I should write to you**: The Thessalonians were well taught about the return of Jesus and other prophetic matters. Paul taught them about **the times and the seasons** regarding the return of Jesus. They had an idea of the prophetic **times** they lived in, and they could discern the **seasons** of the present culture.

> > i. Again, we are impressed that Paul was with the Thessalonians only for a few weeks (Acts 17:2). In that time, he taught them about the prophetic **times and seasons** regarding the return of Jesus. Paul would be surprised that some people today consider the return of Jesus an unimportant teaching.

> > ii. Jesus criticized the religious leaders of His day because they could not *discern the signs of the times* (Matthew 16:1-3). We should also study the Scriptures, and look to the world around us, so we can be aware of the **times and the seasons**.

> > iii. Hiebert on **times** and **seasons**: "The first designates time in its duration, whether a longer or shorter period; the second draws attention to the characteristics of the period. The first deals with the measurement of time, the second with the suitable or critical nature of the time."

b. **The day of the Lord so comes**: With this phrase, Paul quoted a familiar Old Testament idea. The idea behind the phrase **the day of the Lord** is that this is *Gods'* time. Man has his "day," and the Lord has His **day**. In the ultimate sense, **the day of the Lord is fulfilled** with Jesus judging the earth and returning in glory.

> i. It does not refer to a single day, but to a season when God rapidly advances His agenda to the end of the age. **The day of the Lord** "Is a familiar Old Testament expression. It denotes the day when God intervenes in history to judge His enemies, deliver His people, and establish His kingdom." (Hiebert)

c. **For you yourselves know perfectly that the day of the Lord so comes as a thief in the night**: The Thessalonians knew, and had been taught, that they couldn't know the day of Jesus' return. That day would remain unknown, and come as a surprise, **as a thief in the night**. A thief does not announce the exact time of his arrival.

> i. Some take the idea that **the day of the Lord so comes as a thief in the night** to mean that nothing can or should be known about God's prophetic plan for the future. Yet Paul indicated that they *definitely* knew that the time could not be definitely known.

> ii. Paul certainly was not one to set dates in regard to prophecy, and Jesus forbade setting dates when He said *of that day and hour no one knows* (Matthew 24:36). God *wants* this day to be unexpected, but He wants His people to be prepared for the unexpected.

d. **For when they say, "Peace and safety!" then sudden destruction comes upon them**: The unexpected nature of that day will be a tragedy for the unbeliever. They will be lulled to sleep by political and economic conditions, but they will be rudely awakened. They will hear the frightening verdict **"they shall not escape."**

> i. *When "all's well" and "all is safe" are on the lips of men.* (Moffatt)

> ii. This **sudden** coming, in a time when many say **"Peace and safety!"** must be distinct from the coming of Jesus described in Matthew 24:15-35. The coming of Jesus described in Matthew 24:15-35 happens at a time of great global catastrophe, when no one could possibly say **"peace and safety!"** Comparing passages like this shows us that there must be, in some way, *two aspects* to Jesus' Second Coming.

> - One aspect of His coming is at an unexpected hour, the other is positively predicted.
> - One coming is to a "business as usual" world, the other to a world in cataclysm.

- One coming is meeting Him in the air (1 Thessalonians 4:16-17), the other is Him coming with the saints (Zechariah 14:5).

e. **As labor pains upon a pregnant woman**: The phrase **labor pains** suggest both *inevitability* and *unexpectedness*. Jesus used the same idea in Matthew 24:8, when He spoke of calamities preceding the end times as *the beginning of sorrows*, which is literally *the beginning of labor pains*. The idea is both of giving birth to a new age and implying an increase of intensity and frequency in these calamities.

   i. Trapp on **as labor pains upon a pregnant woman**: "1. Certainly; 2. Suddenly; 3. Irresistibly, inevitably."

2. (4-5) The basis for Paul's exhortations.

But you, brethren, are not in darkness, so that this Day should overtake you as a thief. You are all sons of light and sons of the day. We are not of the night nor of darkness.

a. **But you, brethren, are not in darkness**: In addressing their behavior, Paul first simply told the Thessalonian Christians that they should *be* who they *are*. God has made us **sons of the light and sons of the day**. The time when we were **of the night** or **of the darkness** is in the past. So now we simply have to live up to what God has made us.

   i. "In the Semitic languages generally to be a 'son' of something means to be characterized by that thing." (Morris)

b. **That this Day should over take you as a thief**: Paul means that this should *not* happen for the believer who lives according to their nature as a son of **light** and son of the **day**. They will be ready for the return of Jesus Christ.

   i. "Paul is led from a consideration of the day of the Lord to the thought that the Thessalonians have nothing to fear from the coming of that Day. This leads to the further thought that their lives should be in harmony with all that that day stands for." (Morris)

   ii. In some respect, the coming of Jesus will be a surprise for *everybody*, because no one knows the day or the hour (Matthew 24:36). But for Christians who know the *times and the seasons*, it will not be a complete surprise. No one knows the exact hour a thief will come, but some live in a general preparation against thieves. Those who **are not in darkness**, who live as they **are all sons of light and sons of the day**, these are ready for the return of Jesus.

iii. But if we *are* **in darkness** - perhaps caught up in some of the sin Paul warned against previously in this letter - then we are *not* ready and need to make ourselves ready for the return of Jesus.

3. (6-8) Paul's exhortations: be awake, sober, and watchful.

Therefore let us not sleep, as others *do,* but let us watch and be sober. For those who sleep, sleep at night, and those who get drunk are drunk at night. But let us who are of the day be sober, putting on the breastplate of faith and love, and *as* a helmet the hope of salvation.

a. **Therefore let us not sleep**: Because we do not belong to the *night nor of darkness* (1 Thessalonians 5:5), our spiritual condition should never be marked by **sleep**. Spiritually speaking, we need to be active and aware, to **watch and be sober**.

i. **Not sleep**: Paul used a different word here than for the sleep of death mentioned in 1 Thessalonians 4:13. "The word *sleep* is here used metaphorically to denote indifference to spiritual realities on the part of believers. It is a different word than that in 4:13-15 for the sleep of death. It covers all sorts of moral and spiritual laxity or insensibility." (Hiebert)

ii. **Sleep** speaks of so much that belongs to the world (the **others**), but should not belong to Christians:

- Sleep speaks of *ignorance.*
- Sleep speaks of *insensibility.*
- Sleep speaks of *no defense.*
- Sleep speaks of *inactivity.*

iii. In a sermon on this text titled, *Awake! Awake!* Spurgeon showed the folly and tragedy of the sleeping Christian with three powerful pictures:

- A city suffers under the plague, with an official walking the streets crying out, "Bring out the dead! Bring out the dead!" All the while, a doctor with the cure in his pocket *sleeps.*

- A passenger ship reels under a storm and is about to crash on the rocks, bringing near-certain death to the hundreds of passengers – all the while, the captain *sleeps.*

- A prisoner in his cell is about ready to be led to execution; his heart is terrified at the thought of hanging from his neck, terrified of death, and of what awaits him after death. All the while, a man with a letter of pardon for the condemned man sits in another room – and *sleeps*.

iv. **Sober** doesn't mean humorless. It has in mind someone who *knows the proper value of things*, and therefore doesn't get too excited about the things of this world. The person who lives his or her life for fun and entertainment isn't **sober**.

v. In commanding sobriety, Paul didn't have in mind the sort of people who stamp down all enthusiasm and excitement for Jesus, promoting what they think is a more balanced way to live. Paul himself was an enthusiastic follower of Jesus and accused of religious fanaticism. The Roman official Festus thought Paul was mad (Acts 26:24), and the Corinthians thought he was beside himself (2 Corinthians 5:13).

b. **For those who sleep, sleep at night, and those who get drunk are drunk at night**: The opposite of spiritual *watchfulness* is spiritual **sleep**. The opposite of spiritual *sobriety* is to be *spiritually* **drunk**. As Christians we are **of the day**, and so we must **watch and be sober**.

c. **Putting on the breastplate of faith and love, and as a helmet the hope of salvation**: Paul used the images of a soldier's armor to illustrate the idea of *watchfulness*. A soldier is a good example of someone who must **watch and be sober**, and he is *equipped* to do that with his armor.

i. When one compares this description of spiritual armor with that found in Ephesians 6, there is not an exact correlation. This indicates that Paul saw the idea of spiritual armor as a helpful picture, not something rigid in its particular details.

ii. **Faith and love** are represented by **the breastplate** because the **breastplate** covers the vital organs. No solider would ever go to battle without his **breastplate**, and no Christian is equipped to live the Christian life without **faith and love**.

iii. **The hope of salvation** is represented **as a helmet**, because the **helmet** protects the head, which is just as essential as the **breastplate**. **Hope** isn't used in the sense of wishful thinking, but in the sense of a confident expectation of God's hand in the future.

4. (9-10) The security of our future.

For God did not appoint us to wrath, but to obtain salvation through our Lord Jesus Christ, who died for us, that whether we wake or sleep, we should live together with Him.

a. **For God did not appoint us to wrath**: Before we had *the hope of salvation* (1 Thessalonians 5:8), we had an appointment **to wrath**. We no longer have an appointment **to wrath**, but now **to obtain salvation through our Lord Jesus Christ**.

> i. **Wrath**: It is important to understand that Paul means the **wrath** *of God*. We are saved from the world, the flesh, and the devil. But first and foremost, we are rescued from the **wrath** of God, the **wrath** that *we deserve*. Paul's whole context here is the believer's rescue from the **wrath** of God.

> ii. Our appointment **to wrath** was appointed in two ways. First, because of what Adam did to us and the whole human race, we are appointed **to wrath** (Romans 5:14-19). Second, because of our own sin, we are appointed to wrath. When Jesus died on the cross, He stood in our place in our appointment **to wrath** and reschedules us with an appointment **to obtain salvation**. As believers, when we think we are appointed **to wrath**, we show up for an appointment that was cancelled by Jesus.

> iii. **Who died for us**: The idea is that *Jesus died in our place*. Not simply that Jesus died for us in the sense as a favor for us; but that He **died** as a *substitute* for us.

b. **For God did not appoint us to wrath, but to obtain salvation**: Paul put two interested ideas side-by-side here. **Appoint** emphasizes God's sovereignty but **obtain** is a word that emphasizes human effort. Together, they show that the full scope of salvation involves both divine initiative and human effort.

c. **Whether we wake or sleep, we should live together with Him**: Having obtained **salvation through our Lord Jesus**, we will always **live together with Him**. The promise of unity with Jesus can't be broken; no matter if we live or die (**wake or sleep**), we will always be **with Him**.

> i. **He died for us... whether we wake or sleep**: Jesus' death isn't softened by calling it *sleep*, but our death can be called **sleep**. His death was *death*, so that ours would only be **sleep**.

5. (11) Our privilege: comfort one another.

Therefore comfort each other and edify one another, just as you also are doing.

a. **Therefore comfort each other**: Paul again tells us not to *take* comfort, but to *give* **comfort**. If all Christians have a heart to **comfort each other**, then all will be comforted.

b. **And edify one another**: To **edify** means to *build up*. When we have our first interest in building up other Christians, then God will **edify** us. The idea is of a church full of active participants, not passive spectators.

i. "It is clear that in the primitive churches the care of souls was not delegated to an individual officer, or even the more gifted brethren among them; it was a work in which every believer might have a share." (Hiebert)

c. **Just as you also are doing**: It wasn't that there was no **comfort** among the Thessalonians, or as if no one was edified. But they had to *continue* to comfort others, and to do it *more and more*.

B. Urging and exhorting.

1. (12-13) Paul urges them to do three things in regard to their leaders.

And we urge you, brethren, to recognize those who labor among you, and are over you in the Lord and admonish you, and to esteem them very highly in love for their work's sake. Be at peace among yourselves.

a. **Recognize those who labor among you**: Christians are to **recognize** their leaders, and leaders are described in three ways.

i. **Those who labor among you.** Leaders are recognized not by their title but by their *service*. A title is fine; but only if the title is true and if the title describes what that person really is before God and man.

ii. **And are over you in the Lord.** Leaders are recognized as being "**over**" the congregation in the sense of ruling and providing headship, as a shepherd is **over** the sheep. This describes a clear and legitimate order of authority.

iii. **And admonish you.** Leaders are recognized as those who **admonish** the congregation. To **admonish** means "to caution or to reprove gently; to warn." Morris says of this word, "While its tone is brotherly, it is big-brotherly."

iv. "The Greek construction is three participles united under one article, thus indicating that they are not three distinct groups but one class of men discharging a threefold function." (Hiebert)

b. **Esteem them very highly in love**: Christians are to **esteem** their leaders, and to **esteem them very highly in love**. They should do this **for their work's sake**. They don't deserve esteem because of their title, or because of their personality, but because of their labor on behalf of God's people.

i. "Christian ministers, who preach the *whole truth*, and *labour* in the word and doctrine, are entitled to more than *respect*; the apostle commands them to be esteemed, *abundantly*, and *superabundantly*; and this is to be done *in love*." (Clarke)

ii. Paul twice mentions the *work* of ministry and connects it to the respect these servants should have from those they serve. This suggests at least two things:

- If congregants knew and understood the work done by those with spiritual oversight over them, the congregants would appreciate and respect the leaders more.

- Work is an essential aspect of the ministry, and there is no place for a lazy pastor. "In the first place he states that they *labour*. It follows from this that all idle bellies are excluded from the number of pastors." (Calvin)

iii. "The words in Greek carry such an emphasis as cannot well be expressed in English, importing esteem and love to a hyperbole; their love was to be joined with esteem, and esteem with love, and both these to abound and superabound towards them." (Poole)

iv. If a Christian can't **esteem** and **love** their pastor, they should either get on their knees, asking the Holy Spirit to change their heart, or go somewhere else and put themselves under a pastor they do **esteem** and **love**.

c. **Be at peace among yourselves**: With this simple command Paul said Christians should simply put away all their squabbles and arguments. This is a great way to **esteem** and **love** the leaders of your church.

2. (14-15) Paul exhorts them in how to deal with difficult people.

Now we exhort you, brethren, warn those who are unruly, comfort the fainthearted, uphold the weak, be patient with all. See that no one renders evil for evil to anyone, but always pursue what is good both for yourselves and for all.

a. **Now we exhort you**: To **exhort** is to tell someone what they must do, but without sharpness or a critical spirit. It is not rebuke or condemnation, but neither is it merely a suggestion or advice. It is urgent and serious but associated with comfort.

b. **Warn those who are unruly, comfort the fainthearted, uphold the weak, be patient with all**: Paul told the Thessalonians - the people, not only the pastor and leaders - to minister in a variety of ways, depending on the state of the person who needs the ministry. So if someone is **unruly**, the duty of the Christian is to **warn** them. Others need **comfort**, others need to be upheld.

i. The **unruly** are those who are *out of order*, using a military word that describes the soldier who breaks ranks or marches out of step. This is the self-willed person who simply demands to hold his own opinion or preference. These must be warned.

ii. The **fainthearted** are those who, literally, are *small-souled*. By nature or experience they tend to be timid and lack courage. These need comfort – in the sense of assisting strength – to be brought to them.

iii. The **weak** must be upheld and assisted with an eye to building their own strength instead of perpetuating their weakness.

iv. Some see Paul addressing these three groups in earlier passages of 1 Thessalonians. If so, they provide good examples of how to speak to individuals from each category.

- **Unruly**: The idlers of 1 Thessalonians 4:11-12.

- **Fainthearted**: Those anxious about their departed loved ones in 1 Thessalonians 4:14-17.

- **Weak**: Those suffering under temptations to lapse into immorality in 1 Thessalonians 4:2-8.

c. **Be patient with all**: Though different approaches must be taken with different people, Christians must be **patient with all**. This is because true Christianity is shown by its ability to love and help difficult people. We do not look for only perfect people to minister to and to minister with.

d. **See that no one renders evil for evil to anyone**: The Christian never should seek revenge or vengeance, but let God take up our side. Instead, we must **always pursue what is good both for yourselves and for all**. When we have a forgiving heart towards others, not only is it good for them, it is good for ourselves.

i. In the following passage, Paul will write about more spiritual matters such as prayer, thanksgiving, and worship. But before these spiritual or religious matters comes teaching about right relationships. Jesus made it plain that we should get things right with men before we come to worship God (Matthew 5:23-24).

3. (16-18) Regarding their personal worship.

James Moffatt wrote of these verses, "To comment adequately on these diamond drops would be outline a history of the Christian experience in its higher levels."

Rejoice always, pray without ceasing, in everything give thanks; for this is the will of God in Christ Jesus for you.

a. **Rejoice always**: Not only rejoicing in happy things, but in sorrows also. The Christian can **rejoice always** because their joy isn't based in circumstances, but in God. Circumstances change, but God doesn't.

> i. "I am bound to mention among the curiosities of the churches, that I have known many deeply spiritual Christian people who have been afraid to rejoice… Some take such a view of religion that it is to them a sacred duty to be gloomy." (Spurgeon)

> ii. "Turn this book over and see if there be any precept that the Lord has given you in which he has said, 'Groan in the Lord always, and again I say groan.' You may groan if you like. You have Christian liberty for that; but, at the same time, do believe that you have larger liberty to rejoice, for so it is put before you." (Spurgeon)

b. **Pray without ceasing**: Christians are to pray continually. We can't bow our heads, close our eyes, and fold our hands **without ceasing**, but those are *customs* or prayer, not prayer itself. Prayer is communication with God, and we can live each minute of the day in a constant, flowing, conversation with God.

> i. There is significant, important value in a time where we shut out all other distractions and focus on God in a time of closet prayer (Matthew 6:6). But there is also room - and great value - in every-moment-of-the-day fellowship with God.

> ii. There are many valuable implications from this command:
> - The use of the voice is not an essential element in prayer.
> - The posture of prayer is not of primary importance.
> - The place of prayer is not of great importance.
> - The particular time of prayer is not important.
> - A Christian should never be in a place where he *could not* pray.

c. **In everything give thanks**: We don't **give thanks** *for* everything, but **in everything**. We recognize God's sovereign hand is in charge, and not blind fate or chance.

> i. "When joy and prayer are married their first born child is gratitude." (Spurgeon)

d. **For this is the will of God in Christ Jesus for you**: After each one of these exhortations - **rejoice always, pray without ceasing, in everything give thanks** - we are told to do this because it **is the will of God**. The thought isn't "this is God's will, so you *must* do it." The thought is rather "this is God's will, so you *can* do it." It isn't easy to **rejoice always, pray**

without ceasing, and **in everything give thanks**, but we can do it because it is God's will.

4. (19-22) Paul exhorts them in their public worship.

Do not quench the Spirit. Do not despise prophecies. Test all things; hold fast what is good. Abstain from every form of evil.

a. **Do not quench the Spirit**: We can **quench** the fire of the **Spirit** by our doubt, our indifference, our rejection of Him, or by the distraction of others. When people start to draw attention to *themselves*, it is a sure **quench** to **the Spirit**.

> i. "'Quench' properly applies to the putting out of a flame of some sort, as that of a fire (Mark 9:48), or a lamp (Matthew 25:8). This is the only place in the New Testament where it is used in a metaphorical sense." (Morris) Thomas says that the phrase could be more literally translated, "Stop putting out the Spirit's fire."

> ii. Therefore, this command is based on the familiar image of the Holy Spirit as a fire or a flame. Though there is a sense in which fire cannot be created, we can provide the environment in which it can burn brightly. Yet a flame can be extinguished when it is ignored and no longer tended, or when the flame is overwhelmed by something else.

> iii. "And there is a quenching of the Spirit in others as well as ourselves; people may quench it in their ministers by discouraging them, and in one another by bad examples, or reproaching the zeal and forwardness that they see in them." (Poole)

b. **Do not despise prophecies**: We recognize that the Lord speaks to and through His people today, and we learn to be open to His voice. Of course, we always *test* prophecies (following the command to **test all things**), but we do not **despise** prophecies.

> i. It is very possible that prophesy was being despised because individuals were abusing the gift. There were idlers among the Thessalonians (1 Thessalonians 4:11-12), perhaps who spiritualized their idleness with prophecy. There were date-setters and end-times speculators among the Thessalonians (2 Thessalonians 2:1-5), perhaps who backed up their speculations with supposed prophetic authority.

c. **Test all things; hold fast what is good**: Evil and deception can show itself even in a spiritual setting, so it is important for Christians to **test all things**. When the **test** has been made (according to the standard of God's Word and the discernment of spirit among the leaders), we then **hold fast** to **what is good**.

i. Between the time Paul last saw the Thessalonians and the writing of this letter, he had spent time in Berea (Acts 17:10-12). There, the Christians were of a noble character because they heard Paul's preaching and diligently searched the Scriptures to see if what he said was true. Paul wanted the Thessalonians to have more of the heart and mind of the Bereans.

d. **Abstain from every form of evil**: When the testing is made, any aspect of evil must be rejected. This includes evil that may come with a spiritual image.

i. "The term *form* (*eidous*) literally means 'that which is seen,' the external appearance. It points to the external form in which evil presents itself... They are to shun evil in whatever form or appearance it may present itself." (Hiebert)

ii. "The meaning will be 'evil which can be seen,' and not 'that which appears to be evil.'" (Morris)

C. Conclusion.

1. (23-24) Complete sanctification as God's work in us.

Now may the God of peace Himself sanctify you completely; and may your whole spirit, soul, and body be preserved blameless at the coming of our Lord Jesus Christ. He who calls you *is* faithful, who also will do it.

a. **Now may the God of peace Himself sanctify you completely**: The idea behind the word **sanctify** is "to set apart" - to make something different and distinct, breaking old associations and forming a new association. For example, a dress is a dress; but a wedding dress is *sanctified* - set apart for a special, glorious purpose. God wants us to be *set apart* to Him.

i. The emphasis here is on **completely**: "The adjective (*holoeleis*), occurring only here in the New Testament, is a compound of *holos*, 'whole, entire,' and *telos*, 'end.' Its basic connotation is 'wholly attaining the end, reaching the intended goal,' hence has the force of no part being left unreached." (Hiebert)

b. **Himself sanctify you**: Paul made it clear that sanctification is God's work in us. He puts this emphasis in the words **Himself**, in **be preserved**, in **He who calls you is faithful**, and in **who will do it**. This emphasis completes Paul's previous exhortations. In all that he told the Christian to *do* in 1 Thessalonians 4:1 through 5:22, he never intended that they *do* those things in their own power. More Christians are defeated on account of self-reliance than on account of Satanic attack.

i. "The way in which he effects the transition… indicates that it is only in the power of the God on whom he calls that his exhortations can be brought to fruition. 'I have been urging you to do certain things, *but it is only in God's strength that you will be able to do them*." (Morris)

c. **May your whole spirit, soul, and body be preserved blameless**: Paul's use of **spirit, soul, and body** in this passage has led many to adopt what is called a *trichotimist* view of man, believing that man is made up of three distinct parts: **spirit**, **soul**, and **body**.

i. This view has some merit, but also has problems. One might say that Mark 12:30 divides man's nature into four parts (*heart, soul, mind, and strength*), and that 1 Corinthians 7:34 divides man's nature into two parts (*body* and *spirit*). In some passages the terms *soul* and *spirit* seem to be synonymous, other times they seem to be distinct and hard to define precisely. It seems that there are indeed these three different aspects to the human person, yet the specific meaning of *spirit* or *soul* must be determined by the context.

ii. The great Greek scholar Dean Alford described the spirit and the soul as thus:

- "The SPIRIT (*pneuma*) is the highest and distinctive part of man, the immortal."
- "The SOUL is the lower or animal soul, containing the passions and desires which we have in common with the brutes, but which in us is ennobled and drawn up by the *spirit*."

iii. Being the inner, immaterial part of man that may exist apart from spiritual life, the **soul** connects with the world through the senses of the physical body. It connects with God through faith, which might be called the "sense" of the spirit. We tend to think of the spirit being like the soul, but we may also think of it as being more like the body, the vessel of our interaction with the spiritual world.

iv. Because the soul and spirit both have reference to the non-material part of man, they are easily confused. Often an experience intended to build up the **spirit** only blesses the **soul**. There is nothing wrong with soulish excitement and blessing, but there is nothing in it that builds us up spiritually. This is why many Christians go from one exciting experience to another but never really grow *spiritually* - the ministry they receive is *soulish*.

d. **May your whole spirit, soul, and body be preserved**: We may receive this order as inspired. God intends there to be a hierarchy within the human person, ordered first with the spirit, then with the soul, and finally with the body.

i. This is not to say that the body is inherently evil; that contradicts Paul's main thought here, that the *entire* person is set apart and preserved by God, complete in **spirit, soul, and body**. God saves our body as much as our spirit or soul, and the body has a definite and important role in the whole plan of salvation – to be resurrected into a new body.

ii. Yet, God designed the human to live after the order of **spirit, soul, and body** instead of *body, soul, spirit*. We are to sublimate the needs of the *body* to the *soul*, and the needs of both *body and soul* to the needs of the *spirit*.

iii. This is also how God works in us. "Notice the order – spirit, soul, body. The Shechinah of his presence shines in the holy of holies, and thence pours over into the holy place, and so into the outer court, until the very curtains of the body are irradiated with its light." (Meyer)

2. (25-26) A request for prayer and a greeting given.

Brethren, pray for us. Greet all the brethren with a holy kiss.

a. **Brethren, pray for us**: Paul was an apostle, and the Thessalonian church was made up of young Christians. Paul still believed he needed their prayers, so he simply asked, "**pray for us**."

i. "God requires that his people should pray for his ministers; and it is not to be wondered at, if they who pray not for their preachers should receive no benefit from their teaching." (Clarke)

b. **Greet all the brethren with a holy kiss**: The idea is that Paul wants those who *read* the letter to **greet** all the Christians in Thessalonica on his behalf. If he were there in person, he would **greet all the brethren with a holy kiss** himself, but since he was not there, he would send the greeting through this letter.

i. "Apparently at this time the sexes were segregated in the assembly and the men kissed the men and the women the women... When the kiss came to be exchanged between men and women it became the occasion for their critics to charge the Christians with impurity. The resultant embarrassments gave rise to numerous regulations concerning the practice by the early church councils." (Hiebert)

3. (27-28) Conclusion to the letter.

I charge you by the Lord that this epistle be read to all the holy brethren. The grace of our Lord Jesus Christ *be* with you. Amen.

a. **I charge you by the Lord**: Paul used a strong phrase here. It was important that **this epistle be read** among Christians. This is an unusual statement, unique in Paul's letters. Many different reasons have been suggested for why Paul added this phrase at the end of his letter.

- Since this was his first letter, there was as of yet no established custom of the public reading of his letters, and he wanted to make sure the practice was established.

- Since the letter was a substitute for his personal presence, Paul did not want any disappointment at his absence to dampen the spread of the letter.

- Paul wanted to make sure that the church heard the letter first-hand, and not through intermediaries who might misstate his message.

- Perhaps Paul feared that people would look up passages in the letter that spoke to the issues that interested them the most and ignore the other parts.

    i. "And we hence also may prove against the papists, it ought to be made known to the people, even all the holy brethren, and not confined to the clergy; and to be read in their own tongue, for so, without question, was this Epistle read in a language which the people understood." (Poole)

b. **The grace of our Lord Jesus Christ be with you**: Nearly all Paul's letters begin and end with the idea of **grace**. This is also true of almost everything God has to say to His people.

    i. **Grace** is God's unmerited favor, His bestowal of love and acceptance on us because of who He is and what Jesus has done. **Grace** means that He likes us, and all the reasons are in Him. **Grace** means we can stop working for His love and start receiving it.

    ii. It is appropriate that this letter – the first of Paul's preserved correspondence to the churches – this letter full of love, encouragement, and instruction, end on a note of **grace**.

    iii. "Whatever God has to say to us – and in all the New Testament letters there are things that search the heart and make it quake – begins and ends with grace... All that God has been to man in Jesus Christ is summed up in it: all His gentleness and beauty, all His tenderness and patience, all the holy passion of His love, is gathered up in grace. What more could one soul wish for another than that the grace of the Lord Jesus Christ should be with it?" (Denney, cited in Morris)

2 Thessalonians 1 - The Godly Character of a Persecuted Church

A. Encouragement for persecuted Christians.

1. (1-2) A greeting from Paul and his associates.

Paul, Silvanus, and Timothy, To the church of the Thessalonians in God our Father and the Lord Jesus Christ: Grace to you and peace from God our Father and the Lord Jesus Christ.

a. **Paul, Silvanus, and Timothy**: Paul traveled with these men and together they contributed to this letter. Though the name **Paul** is listed first, both **Silvanus** and **Timothy** were his trusted companions.

i. **Silvanus** (also known as *Silas*) was a long and experienced companion of Paul. He traveled with Paul on his second missionary journey and was imprisoned and set free with Paul in the Philippian jail (Acts 16:19-27). When Paul first came to Thessalonica, Silas came with him (Acts 17:1-9), so the Thessalonians knew **Silvanus** well. He also collaborated with Paul on the first letter to the Thessalonians (1 Thessalonians 1:1).

ii. **Timothy** was a resident of Lystra, a city in the province of Galatia (Acts 16:1-3). He was the son of a Greek father (Acts 16:1), and a Jewish mother named Eunice (2 Timothy 1:5). From his youth, he had been taught in the Scriptures by his mother and grandmother (2 Timothy 1:5; 3:15). Timothy was a trusted companion and associate of Paul, and he accompanied Paul on many of his missionary journeys. Paul sent Timothy to the Thessalonians on a previous occasion (1 Thessalonians 3:2). With Silvanus, Timothy was also a collaborator on Paul's first letter to the Thessalonians (1 Thessalonians 1:1).

b. **To the church of the Thessalonians**: Paul himself founded the church in Thessalonica on his second missionary journey (Acts 17:1-9). He was only in the city a short time because he was forced out by enemies of the

Gospel. But **the church of the Thessalonians** left behind was alive and active. Paul's deep concern for this young church, which he had to suddenly leave, prompted this letter – following after the letter of 1 Thessalonians.

c. **Grace to you and peace from God our Father and the Lord Jesus Christ**: Paul brought his customary greeting to the Thessalonian Christians, hailing them in the **grace** and **peace** of God the Father.

> i. Morris cites Bicknell: "The Greek makes it plain that the Father and Christ are one source. It is remarkable that even at this early date the Son is placed side by side with the Father as the fount of divine grace, without any need of comment."

2. (3-4) Paul's thanks and boasting about the Thessalonians.

We are bound to thank God always for you, brethren, as it is fitting, because your faith grows exceedingly, and the love of every one of you all abounds toward each other, so that we ourselves boast of you among the churches of God for your patience and faith in all your persecutions and tribulations that you endure,

a. **We are bound to thank God always for you**: For Paul, the giving of thanks for God's great work was an *obligation* - he was **bound** to do so, and it was **fitting**, because of the work God did in the Thessalonian Christians.

> i. Paul's wording here is strong. "Paul has already written a very warm letter, containing some passages of high praise for the Thessalonian church. It is probable that in the subsequent communications that they had had with him (whether by letter, or by word of mouth) that had said that they were not worthy of such praise. Paul strongly maintains that his words had not been too strong." (Morris)

> ii. "It is your duty to praise him. You are bound by the bonds of his love as long as you live to bless his name. It is meet and comely that you should do so. It is not only a pleasurable exercise, but it is the absolute duty of the Christian life to praise God." (Spurgeon)

b. **Because your faith grows exceedingly**: Paul thanked God because the Thessalonians had:

- **Exceedingly** growing **faith**.
- Abounding **love**.
- **Patience and faith in all... persecutions and tribulations**.

> i. This **faith** and **love**, thriving in the midst of **persecutions and tribulations**, made Paul **boast** of the Thessalonians to other churches.

ii. "His verb for 'groweth exceedingly' is an unusual one (here only in the Greek Bible), and gives the thought of a very vigorous growth." (Morris)

iii. Spurgeon explained how to get a strong and growing faith: "By that means you are to grow. This is so with faith. Do all you can, and then do a little more; and when you can do that, then do a little more than you can. Always have something in hand that is greater then your present capacity. Grow up to it, and when you have grown up to it, grow more."

c. **So that we ourselves**: This "is a very emphatic expression, much more emphatic than we would have expected in such a connection. It implies a strong contrast." (Morris) The idea is that though it was unusual for someone who planted a church to glory in its success and health, Paul was so impressed by what God was doing among the Thessalonians even Paul took the liberty to glory in that work.

i. "By these words Paul shows us that we are under an obligation to give thanks to God not only when He does us a kindness, but also when we consider the kindness which He has shown towards our brethren." (Calvin)

B. The persecuted Thessalonians and their persecutors.

1. (5-7) The persecution and tribulation of the Thessalonians set the righteousness of God on display.

Which is manifest evidence of the righteous judgment of God, that you may be counted worthy of the kingdom of God, for which you also suffer; since *it is* a righteous thing with God to repay with tribulation those who trouble you, and to *give* you who are troubled rest with us when the Lord Jesus is revealed from heaven with His mighty angels,

a. **Which is manifest evidence of the righteous judgment of God**: God's **righteous judgment** was at work among the Thessalonians, beginning at the house of God (1 Peter 4:17), and purifying them as followers of Jesus. The good result - showing them **worthy of the kingdom of God** - was **manifest evidence** that God was good in allowing them to suffer the *persecutions and tribulations* described in 2 Thessalonians 1:4.

i. We usually think that God is *absent* when we suffer, and that our suffering calls God's righteous judgment into question. Paul took the exact opposite position and insisted that the Thessalonians' suffering was **evidence of the righteous judgment of God**. Where suffering is coupled with righteous endurance, God's work is done. The fires of persecution and tribulation were like the purifying fires of a refiner, burning away the dross from the gold, bringing forth a pure, precious metal.

ii. The idea behind **counted worthy** is not "seen as worthy" but "reckoned as worthy" as in a judicial decree. Paul's prayer was that the worthiness of Jesus may be accounted to the Thessalonian Christians.

b. **Since it is a righteous thing with God**: Many people question the righteousness of God's judgment. They believe that God's love and His judgment contradict each other. But God's judgment is based on the great spiritual principle that it is a **righteous thing with God to repay** those who do evil. Since God is **righteous**, He will **repay** *all evil*, and it will all be judged and accounted for either at the cross or in hell.

i. The judgment of God means that there is nothing unimportant in my life. Everything is under the eye of the God I must answer to.

ii. "A world in which justice was not done at last would not be God's world at all." (Hiebert)

c. **To repay with tribulation those who trouble you**: God was also shown as **righteous** when those who persecuted the Thessalonians were repaid with **tribulation** according to their evil works. They probably believed they did God a favor when they persecuted the Christians, but the **righteous** God would **repay** them and not *reward* them.

i. "Often retribution is pictured as overtaking men in the world to come, but there are not wanting passages which indicated that it may operate in the here and now (e.g., Rom. 1:24, 26, 28)." (Morris)

ii. We can see a statement like 2 Thessalonians 1:6 in much the same context as those passages in the Psalms where the writer happily wishes ill upon his enemies – they are a prayer of entrusting the judgment of these enemies to *God*, instead of personally taking the initiative.

iii. The **tribulation** upon these persecutors of God's people is not like a purifying fire. It is like the fire of a pure and holy judgment.

d. **And to give you who are troubled rest**: The Thessalonian Christians were persecuted and had tribulation; and God used it for His glory. But the time of persecution would not last. A day of **rest** is promised for every believer.

2. (8-10) The coming day of judgment for both the persecuted and their persecutors.

In flaming fire taking vengeance on those who do not know God, and on those who do not obey the gospel of our Lord Jesus Christ. These shall be punished with everlasting destruction from the presence of the

Lord and from the glory of His power, when He comes, in that Day, to be glorified in His saints and to be admired among all those who believe, because our testimony among you was believed.

a. **In flaming fire taking vengeance**: This is what the day of judgment will be like for those who persecuted the Thessalonians. For the persecutors, *those* **who do not know God**, and **those who do not obey the gospel of our Lord Jesus**, that will be a day of **vengeance** and **everlasting destruction**.

i. **In flaming fire**: It isn't the fire that makes hell what it is. In the fiery furnace, the three Jewish young men were completely comfortable, as long as the Lord was with them in the fire (Daniel 3). What truly characterizes hell is that there, people are **from the presence of the Lord**, in the sense of being apart from anything *good* or *blessed* in God's presence. **From the presence of the Lord** sums up the Bible's understanding of hell. Nothing must be said more about its horrors, other than hell will be completely devoid of God and every aspect of His character, except one: His unrelenting holy justice.

ii. It is not wrong for God to take **vengeance**; we understand this when we understand what the word means in the ancient Greek language. "The word rendered 'vengeance' has no associations of vindictiveness. It is a compound based on the same root as the word rendered 'righteous' in vv. 5, 6, and it has the idea of a firm administration of unwavering justice." (Morris) The idea is the application of *full justice* on the offender; nothing more and nothing less.

iii. **Everlasting destruction**: We must not be moved from the idea that the punishment of the wicked is **everlasting**. As the blessings of heaven are eternal, the penalty of hell is also eternal. "The perpetual duration of this death is proved from the fact that its opposite is the glory of Christ. This is eternal and has no end." (Calvin)

b. **To be glorified in His saints and to be admired among all those who believe**: For the persecuted **saints**, those **who believe**, they will have God **glorified in** them on that **Day**, and they will see and admire Jesus more than ever.

i. "To raise up such a number of poor, sinful, despicable worms out of the dust into such a sublime state of glory and dignity, will be admirable." (Poole)

ii. We will admire what God has done in others and in us. "Those who look upon the saints will feel a sudden wonderment of sacred delight; they will be startled with the surprising glory of the Lord's work in them; 'We thought He would do great things, but this! This surpasseth conception!' Every saint will be a wonder to himself. 'I thought my bliss would be great, but not like this!' All his brethren will be a wonder to the perfected believer. He will say, 'I thought the saints would be perfect, but I never imagined such a transfiguration of excessive glory would be put upon each of them. I could not have imagined my Lord to be so good and gracious.'" (Spurgeon)

c. **Because our testimony among you was believed**: This shows the difference between one destined for judgment and one destined for glory. The difference is belief in the message Paul preached (**our testimony**), the simple Gospel of Jesus Christ.

> i. Paul knew what it was like to be transformed from a persecutor to the persecuted. He believed the **testimony** of the Gospel of Jesus Christ, and it changed his life.

3. (11-12) Paul's prayer for the Thessalonians.

Therefore we also pray always for you that our God would count you worthy of *this* calling, and fulfill all the good pleasure of *His* goodness and the work of faith with power, that the name of our Lord Jesus Christ may be glorified in you, and you in Him, according to the grace of our God and the Lord Jesus Christ.

a. **Therefore we also pray always**: Since the Thessalonian Christians were in the midst of persecution and tribulation, they needed prayer. Here, Paul assured them that he and his associates **pray always** for them.

b. **That our God would count you worthy of this calling**: God gives Christians a high **calling**, mentioned in the previous sentence. The **calling** is to see Him glorified in us at His coming. Paul rightly prays that the Thessalonians may be counted **worthy of this calling**, and he shows ways to fulfill this calling.

> i. We live worthy of His call when we **fulfill all the good pleasure of His goodness**, living lives *touched* by **His goodness**, and *displaying* **His goodness**.

> ii. We live worthy of His call when we **fulfill ... the work of faith with power**, believing on Jesus and seeing His work done all around us by faith.

> iii. We live worthy of His call when **the name of our Lord Jesus Christ** is **glorified in** us. We understand that this means more than the **name of our Lord Jesus** as a word, but also as a representation of His character.

iv. We live worthy of His call when we are glorified **in Him**, when He alone is our source of glory and exaltation, and who we are in Jesus is more important than who we are in anything else.

c. **According to the grace of our God and the Lord Jesus Christ**: This great work of living worthy of His calling can only happen **according to the grace of God**. It happens by His power, favor, and acceptance in work in us, moving along our will and cooperation.

2 Thessalonians 2 - The Coming of That Day

A. Instruction regarding the coming of Jesus.

1. (1-2) Paul's comfort to the troubled Thessalonians and their question.

Now, brethren, concerning the coming of our Lord Jesus Christ and our gathering together to Him, we ask you, not to be soon shaken in mind or troubled, either by spirit or by word or by letter, as if from us, as though the day of Christ had come.

a. **Concerning the coming of our Lord Jesus Christ and our gathering together to Him**: Paul here addressed questions raised by his first letter, where he instructed the Thessalonians about the catching away of the church to be with Jesus (1 Thessalonians 4:16-18).

i. The challenge in understanding this chapter comes from the fact that it is a *supplement* to what Paul has already taught the Thessalonians in words, and we don't know exactly what Paul said to the them. Yet the ideas are clear enough if carefully pieced together.

b. **Concerning the coming of our Lord Jesus Christ and our gathering together to Him**: Paul clearly wrote of the return of Jesus, but the wording here implies a difference between **the coming** and **our gathering**. This strongly suggests that there are essentially two comings of Jesus. One coming is *for* His church (as described clearly in 1 Thessalonians 4:16-18), and the other coming is *with* His church, to judge a rebellious world.

i. "They are two parts of one great event." (Morris)

ii. Hiebert shows how the grammar of the ancient Greek in 2 Thessalonians 2:1 shows this: "The government of the two nouns under one article makes it clear that one event, viewed under two complimentary aspects, is thought of."

iii. This is completely consistent with other passages of Scripture that indicate that there must be two aspects of Jesus' second coming, and the aspects must be separated by some appreciable period of time.

- Different world conditions are described (Matthew 24:37-42, Matthew 24:21, Revelation 6:15-16).

- Different manners of Jesus' return are described (1 Thessalonians 4:16-17, Revelation 19:11, 14-15, 21).

- Different scenarios regarding the predictability of the date of Jesus' return are established (Matthew 24:36, Daniel 12:11).

c. **We ask you, not to be soon shaken in mind or troubled**: Apparently, a misunderstanding of Paul's teaching (or an incorrect application of it) had caused the Thessalonians to be **shaken in mind** and **troubled**. Here Paul used a strong wording, speaking of both a *sudden jolt* (**shaken in mind**) and a continuing state of upset (**troubled**). Their fears centered on the idea that **the day of Christ had** [already] **come**.

> i. "The word *to be shaken*, signifies to be agitated as a ship at sea in a storm, and strongly marks the confusion and distress which the Thessalonians had felt in their false apprehension of this coming of Christ." (Clarke)

> ii. A preferred manuscript reading of 2 Thessalonians 2:2 has *the day of the Lord* rather than **the day of Christ**. The *day of the Lord* is a concept with a rich Old Testament background, and was mentioned in Paul's previous letter to the Thessalonians (1 Thessalonians 5:2). It is not a single day, but a period associated with God's outpouring of judgment and the deliverance of God's people. A significant aspect of the *day of the Lord* is the Great Tribulation described in Matthew 24:1-31.

d. **As though the day of Christ had come**: Some translations have *that the day of Christ is at hand*, such as the King James Version. But the translation in the New King James Version (and other modern translations) is preferred. The Thessalonians were not afraid that the **day of Christ** was *coming*, but that they were *in it*.

> i. "The verb does not really mean *to be at hand*, but rather *to be present*." (Morris) The notable Greek commentator Dean Alford translates the passage, "**To the effect that the day of the Lord is present**; not, '*is at hand*': the verb used here occurs six times in the New Testament, and always in the sense of *being present*; in two of those places, Romans 8:38, 1 Corinthians 3:22, *the things present* are distinguished expressly from *the things to come*."

> ii. From this, it is obvious that the **day of Christ** had not been *completed*. Paul will go on to demonstrate that it also had not yet *dawned*, because the Thessalonians were afraid that they were in the Great Tribulation (the *day of the Lord*), and feared that they had missed the rapture. But

2 Thessalonians 2   79

Paul will demonstrate that they are not in the **day of Christ**; because if they were, then certain signs would be present.

iii. It is important to notice that the Thessalonians would be **shaken** or **troubled** by the thought of being in the Great Tribulation *only* if they had been taught by Paul that they would *escape* that period through the rapture. Otherwise they would, in a sense, *welcome* the Great Tribulation as a necessary prelude to the Second Coming. But Paul had clearly taught them that they would escape God's judgment on this earth during the period known as the *day of the Lord* or the **day of Christ** (1 Thessalonians 4:14-18).

e. **Either by spirit or by word or by letter**: Perhaps the troubling word had come through a misguided prophecy (**spirit or by word**). Or perhaps some other leader wrote the Thessalonians a **letter** teaching that they were already in the **day of Christ**. Either way, they were upset at the idea that they had somehow missed the rapture.

i. "The teaching of the Apostles was, and of the Holy Spirit in all ages has been, that the day of the Lord *is at hand*. But these Thessalonians imagined it to be already come." (Alford)

2. (3) Signs marking the coming day.

Let no one deceive you by any means; for *that Day will not come* unless the falling away comes first, and the man of sin is revealed, the son of perdition,

a. **For that Day will not come**: Paul will not describe events which must *precede* the rapture, but events that are *concrete evidence* of the Great Tribulation - **the day of Christ**. In this sense, one cannot be *certain* the **day of Christ** (the Great Tribulation) has come unless these signs are present.

i. This phrase is not in the original text, but is very appropriately added. Alford says of the phrase, **for that day will not come**: "So A.V. supplies, rightly. There does not seem to have been any intention on the part of the Apostle to fill up the ellipsis: it supplies itself in the reader's mind."

b. **Unless the falling away comes first**: The ancient Greek wording for **falling away** indicates a *rebellion* or a *departure*. Bible scholars debate if it refers to an apostasy among those who once followed God, or a general worldwide rebellion. In fact, Paul may have both in mind, because there is evidence of each in the end times (1 Timothy 4:1-3, 2 Timothy 3:1-5 and 4:3-4). Nevertheless, Paul's point is clear: "You are worried that we are in the Great Tribulation and that you missed the rapture. But you can know that we are *not* in the Great Tribulation, because we have not yet seen **the falling away** that **comes first**."

> i. **The falling away**: The article "the" makes it even more significant. This is not *a* **falling away**, but *the* **falling away**, the great and final rebellion.

> ii. Some have suggested that the idea behind **falling away** is really *a departure*, in the sense of the rapture of the church. But *a departure* implies that the one leaving does so of his own accord and initiative, and this is not the case with the catching away of the church. In addition, the ancient Greek word in the New Testament (Acts 21:21, *forsake*) or in the Septuagint, always implies something sinful and negative.

> iii. The idea of a great end-times apostasy also does not contradict the idea of a great end-times revival. Some Christians doubt the idea of great revival in the last days, or even welcome apostasy believing it signals the end. But just as the Book of Revelation describes great rejection of Jesus during the Great Tribulation (Revelation 9:20-21 and 17:2-6) *and* great acceptance of Him (Revelation 7:9-14), the two can stand side-by-side.

c. **And the man of sin is revealed**: Before the Great Tribulation can be identified with certainty, a particular person – known as **the man of sin**, – must be **revealed**. Paul's point is clear: "You are worried that we are in the Great Tribulation and that you missed the rapture. But you can know that we are *not* in the Great Tribulation, because we have not yet seen **the man of sin ... revealed**."

> i. The most traditional understanding of this **man of sin** is to say that he is not an individual, but a system or an office. Historically, Protestant interpreters have seen the **man of sin** to be the succession of popes. Calvin thought this way: "Paul, however, is not speaking of one individual, but of a kingdom that was to be seized by Satan for the purpose of setting up a seat of abomination in the midst of God's temple. This we see accomplished in popery."

> ii. However, there is *no* good reason to see this **man of sin** to be other than what the plainest meaning is here – an individual who will come to great prominence in the very last days. This was how it was understood in the earliest days of Christianity. "The *fathers* understood the *Antichrist* to be intended, but of this person they seemed to have formed no specific idea." (Clarke)

- Daniel described an individual person: *The prince who is to come* (Daniel 9:26), the *king of fierce countenance* (Daniel 8:23), the *willful king* (Daniel 11:36-45).

- Jesus described an individual person: The one who comes *in his own name* (John 5:43).

- We are not surprised that Paul described this **man of sin** as an individual person, *not* as a system or an office.

iii. This **man of sin** is a prominent figure in the Bible, and the ultimate personification of the *spirit of the Antichrist* spoken of in 1 John 4:2-3. He will no doubt live many years before the Great Tribulation, but he will only be **revealed** as the **man of sin** during that period. The idea behind the title **man of sin** is that "Sin has such absolute domination over him that he seems to be the very embodiment of it." (Hiebert)

d. **Son of perdition**: **Perdition** means *destruction*, the complete loss of well-being. It is really the opposite of *salvation*. To call him the **son of perdition** means his character is marked by this destruction. Moffatt says the phrase "**son of perdition**" essentially means *the doomed one*.

3. (4) What the *man of sin* does.

Who opposes and exalts himself above all that is called God or that is worshiped, so that he sits as God in the temple of God, showing himself that he is God.

a. **Who opposes and exalts himself above all that is called God or is worshipped**: The *man of sin* demands worship for himself that belongs to God only (Luke 4:8). This demand for worship is also described in Revelation 13:1-6.

i. "He *stands against* and *exalts* himself *above* all Divine authority, and above every *object of adoration*, and every *institution* relative to Divine worship." (Clarke)

ii. Understanding the strength and breadth of this statement shows us that saying that the Antichrist is the Pope is far too simplistic. He will sponsor a religion that does not tolerate the worship of anyone or anything except himself. The apostate Roman Catholic Church may be part of this end-times religion, but it will not encompass it.

iii. "Notice, that the meaning of these words cannot by any probability be fulfilled by any one who, as the Pope, creates objects of worship, and thus (by inference merely) makes himself greater than the objects which he creates: but it is required that this Antichrist should *set*

HIMSELF *up as an object of worship*, above, and as superior to, 'everyone that is called God or worshipped.'" (Alford)

b. **So that he sits as God in the temple of God**: The man of sin's demand for worship will be so extreme, he will set himself up as God in the temple at Jerusalem, demanding this blasphemous worship from everyone (Revelation 13:14-15 and Matthew 24:15, 21, 29-31).

> i. **The temple of God**: That this is a literal temple is clear from the text, and has been understood as such by even the earliest Christians. "But when this Antichrist shall have devastated all things in this world, he will reign for three years and six months, and sit in the temple at Jerusalem; and then the Lord will come from heaven in the clouds, in the glory of the Father, sending this man and those who follow him into the lake of fire; but bringing in for the righteous the times of the kingdom." (Irenaeus, writing in the late second century)

> ii. The literal understanding of Paul's words is also supported by the fact that when he wrote this letter, something similar to this *almost* happened in the recent past. "The recent attempt of Caligula to erect a statue of himself in the Temple at Jerusalem may have furnished a trait for Paul's delineation of the future Deceiver; the fearful impiety of this outburst had sent a profound shock through Judaism, which would be felt by Jewish Christians as well." (Moffatt)

c. **He sits as God in the temple**: The specific ancient Greek word for **temple** indicates *the most holy place* and not the temple as a whole. "It is not that he enters the temple precincts: he invades the most sacred place and there takes his seat. His action is itself a claim to deity." (Morris) This is the ultimate blasphemy that results in certain judgment, the *abomination of desolation* spoken of by both Daniel and Jesus.

> i. The prophet Daniel told us the Antichrist will break his covenant with the Jews and bring sacrifice and offerings to an end; that the Antichrist will defile the temple by setting something abominable there (Daniel 9:27, 11:31, and 12:11).

> ii. Jesus said to look for an abomination standing in the holy place, which would be the pivotal sign that the season of God's wrath was upon the earth (Matthew 24:15-16 and 24:21).

> iii. "Any man may be satisfied that St. Paul alluded to Daniel's description, because he has not only borrowed the same ideas, but has even adopted some of the phrases and expressions." (Clarke)

d. **Showing himself that he is God**: The man of sin is truly an *Anti*-Christ. Satan has planned the career of the man of sin to mirror the ministry of Jesus.

- Both Jesus and the man of sin have a coming (2 Thessalonians 2:1 and 2:9).

- Both Jesus and the man of sin are revealed (2 Thessalonians 1:7 and 2:3).

- Both Jesus and the man of sin have a gospel (2 Thessalonians 2:10-11).

- Both Jesus and the man of sin say that they alone should be worshipped (2 Thessalonians 2:4).

- Both Jesus and the man of sin have support for their claims by miraculous works (2 Thessalonians 2:9).

  i. Clearly, the man of sin is Satan's parody of the true Messiah. Yet in the end, the *man of sin* can only show *himself* that he is God. The coming of Jesus and the judgment of God will make it clear that the man of sin is not God at all.

4. (5-8) What restrains the coming of this *man of sin*.

Do you not remember that when I was still with you I told you these things? And now you know what is restraining, that he may be revealed in his own time. For the mystery of lawlessness is already at work; only He who now restrains *will do so* until He is taken out of the way. And then the lawless one will be revealed, whom the Lord will consume with the breath of His mouth and destroy with the brightness of His coming.

a. **When I was still with you I told you these things**: Paul was only with the Thessalonians a few weeks (Acts 17:1-10). But Paul thought it important to teach these brand new Christians about Biblical prophecy, and he taught them in some detail.

b. **And now you know what is restraining**: For now, Satan and the *man of sin* are being restrained. The principle of their working is now present (**the mystery of lawlessness is already at work**). But at the right time, the Holy Spirit (**He who restrains**) who restrains their full revelation will be taken out of the way.

c. **Taken out of the way**: We should not think that the Holy Spirit would *leave* the earth during the Great Tribulation. He will be present on the earth during the Great Tribulation because many are saved, sealed, and serve God during this period (Revelation 7:3-14 and 14:1-5), and this can't happen without the ministry of the Holy Spirit. The Holy Spirit is **taken out of the way**, not removed.

> i. "The phrase is used of any person or thing which is taken out of the way, whether by death or other removal." (Alford)
>
> ii. Some see this as the end of a dispensation: "The special presence of the Spirit as the indweller of saints will terminate abruptly at the *parousia* as it began abruptly at Pentecost. Once the body of Christ has been caught away to heaven, the Spirit's ministry will revert back to what he did for believers during the Old Testament period." (Thomas)

d. **The mystery of lawlessness is already at work**: This great principle of evil is already present in the world. It will be ultimately unveiled in the man of sin, but he does not introduce a *new* wickedness into the world, only an intensity of prior wickedness.

> i. Right now, this **lawlessness** is a **mystery** – that it is, it can only be seen and understood by revelation. Otherwise it is hidden. "It is not open sin and wickedness, but dissembled piety, specious errors, wickedness under a form of godliness cunningly managed, that is here meant." (Poole)

e. **And then the lawless one will be revealed**: Paul states two certain facts about the man of sin, here called **the lawless one**. First, it is certain that the **lawless one will be revealed** when the Holy Spirit removes His restraint. Second, it is certain that the **lawless one** will be destroyed by the mere **brightness** of Jesus at **His coming**.

> i. Paul probably has Isaiah 11:4 in mind: *He shall strike the earth with the rod of His mouth, and with the breath of His lips He shall slay the wicked.* The Isaiah passage refers to the LORD – to Yahweh – but Paul freely used it of Jesus, recognizing that Jesus is Yahweh.
>
> ii. Whoever the *man of sin* is, he has not had his career yet. We know this because at the end of his career, the *man of sin* is destroyed by Jesus Christ Himself.

5. (9-12) The character and strategy of the *man of sin*.

The coming of the *lawless one* is according to the working of Satan, with all power, signs, and lying wonders, and with all unrighteous deception among those who perish, because they did not receive the love of the truth, that they might be saved. And for this reason God will send them strong delusion, that they should believe the lie, that they all may be condemned who did not believe the truth but had pleasure in unrighteousness.

a. **The coming of the lawless one is according to the working of Satan**: The Antichrist will come with **power**, with **signs** and with **lying wonders**. But all of this **is according to the working of Satan**, as described in Revelation 13:13-17.

> i. If someone has spiritual **power**, **signs**, or **wonders**, those are not enough to prove they are from God. Satan can perform his own powerful works, either through deception or through his own resources of power.

> ii. "He is Satan's messiah, an infernal caricature of the true messiah." (Moffatt)

b. **Among those who perish**: However, the deception can only take root in those who **do not receive the love of the truth**. These people are ready for the deception of the Antichrist, because they *want* a lie, and **God will send them a strong delusion**.

> i. **God will send them**: In the end, the Antichrist is only God's messenger. God has judgment to bring, and He will **send ... a strong delusion** through the Antichrist. God will not *force* this **delusion** on anyone, but those who **do not receive the love of the truth** will receive this **strong delusion.**

> ii. Alford translates: *God is sending to them the working of delusion in order that they should believe the falsehood.*

> iii. "They were first deluded, which was their sin; and God sends them strong delusion, and that is their punishment." (Poole)

c. **That they should believe the lie**: Specifically, God sends them *the* **lie**. This isn't just *any* **lie**, but *the* **lie**, the lie that has enthralled the human race since Adam. This is **the lie** that God is not God, and that we are or can be gods.

> i. "His point is that the last pseudo-Messiah or anti-Christ will embody all that is profane and blasphemous, every conceivable element of impiety; and that, instead of being repudiated, he will be welcome by Jews as well as pagans." (Moffatt)

d. **That they all may be condemned who did not believe the truth but had pleasure in unrighteousness**: As God gives rebellious man the lie he desires, it isn't out of His generosity. Instead, it shows God's judgment on those who reject the truth. As Romans 1 points out, in judgment God may give a man up to the depravity of his heart, to his **pleasure in unrighteousness**.

i. "They think that they are acting in defiance of Him. But in the end they find that those very acts in which they expressed their defiance were the vehicle of their punishment." (Morris)

B. Encouragement for last days believers.

1. (13-14) Paul gives thanks for God's work in the Thessalonians

But we are bound to give thanks to God always for you, brethren beloved by the Lord, because God from the beginning chose you for salvation through sanctification by the Spirit and belief in the truth, to which He called you by our gospel, for the obtaining of the glory of our Lord Jesus Christ.

a. **But we are bound to give thanks**: Paul repeats his idea from 2 Thessalonians 1:3, that he was obligated to thank God for His work in the Thessalonians, in light of the greatness of that work.

b. **Brethren beloved by the Lord**: Paul is first thankful that they are **beloved by the Lord**. God's love for us is the primary motivation for all His work in and through us.

c. **Because God from the beginning chose you for salvation**: Paul also praised the sovereign choice of God in bringing the Thessalonians to salvation. God's choice was **from the beginning**. Before they chose God, He **chose** them, and He **chose** them for **salvation through sanctification**.

i. "From the beginning! Who shall compute the contents of the vast unknown abyss, which is comprehended in that phrase? The beginning of creation was preceded by the anticipation of Redemption, and the love of God to all who were one with Christ." (Meyer)

ii. **Salvation through sanctification**: The two go together. Those who claim to be chosen but lack evidence of **sanctification** (separation *from* the world and *unto* God) are on shaky ground. We can't see if a person *is chosen*, but we can see if they are *sanctified*.

iii. "Had it been possible for you to have had salvation without sanctification, it would have been a curse to you instead of a blessing. If such a thing were possible, I cannot conceive of a more lamentable condition than for a man to, have the happiness of salvation without the holiness of it; happily, it is not possible. If you could be saved from the consequences of sin, but not from the sin itself, and its power and pollution, it would be no blessing to you." (Spurgeon)

d. **By the Spirit and belief in the truth**: God's work of sanctification uses two great forces, the **Spirit** and the **belief in the truth**. The Spirit of God and the Word of God are *essential* to our **sanctification**.

e. **To which He called you by our gospel**: The call for this salvation comes through the **gospel**, the Gospel Paul preached (*we preach Christ crucified*, 1 Corinthians 1:23), and the Gospel that will enable us to obtain the glory of Jesus.

f. **For the obtaining of the glory of our Lord Jesus Christ**: This is the same glory John wrote of in 1 John 3:2 - *we know that when He is revealed, we shall be like Him, for we shall see Him as He is.*

2. (15) An exhortation to stand fast.

Therefore, brethren, stand fast and hold the traditions which you were taught, whether by word or our epistle.

a. **Therefore, brethren, stand fast**: **Therefore** means that Paul wants us to consider what he has written up to this point. In this letter, he has given compelling reasons why Christians must **stand fast** and not be moved.

- **Stand fast** because the current distress (the *persecutions and tribulations* described in 2 Thessalonians 1:4).

- **Stand fast** because of the coming judgment of this world (*in flaming fire taking vengeance*, 2 Thessalonians 1:8).

- **Stand fast** because of the strength of coming deception (*all power, signs, and lying wonders*, 2 Thessalonians 2:9).

- **Stand fast** because of our glorious destiny (*the glory of our Lord Jesus*, 2 Thessalonians 2:14).

b. **Stand fast and hold the traditions**: The command to **stand fast** implies a *location*, and this tells us what Christians must **stand fast** upon. They must keep standing on God's Word, delivered both by the authoritative word of the apostles (**by word**) and the letters of the apostles (**our epistle**).

i. **Traditions**: The Bible recognizes that **traditions** can be a dangerous feature of religious systems (Matthew 15:2-3) or the traditions of man (Colossians 2:8). But Paul has in mind the *apostolic* **traditions** preserved for us in the record of the New Testament.

ii. "The word *paradoseis*, which we render tradition, signifies anything delivered in the way of teaching; and here most obviously means the doctrines delivered by the apostle to the Thessalonians; whether in his preaching, private conversation, or by these letters." (Clarke)

iii. It is only this anchor of God's Word that can enable us to **stand fast** under the weight of our present tribulation, and the weight of our coming glory.

3. (16-17) A prayer for the Thessalonians.

Spurgeon preached five separate sermons on these wonderful verses.

Now may our Lord Jesus Christ Himself, and our God and Father, who has loved us and given *us* everlasting consolation and good hope by grace, comfort your hearts and establish you in every good word and work.

a. **Who has loved us**: Before Paul asked God to do something specific for the Thessalonians, he remembered all God *had* done for them. God has **loved** them, and gave them **everlasting consolation** and **good hope by grace**.

i. In our intercession and petition, we do well to remember God's past faithfulness and present blessing. His faithfulness in the past is a promise of His faithfulness for the future.

ii. "*God has given us much*, and all his past gifts are pleas for more gifts. Men do not plead so. The beggar in the street cannot say, 'Give me a penny to-day because you gave me one yesterday,' else we might reply, 'That is the reason why I should not give you any more.' But when dealing with God, this is a good plea." (Spurgeon)

b. **Comfort your hearts and establish you**: Paul asked God to do two things in the Thessalonian Christians. First, he wanted God to **comfort** their **hearts**. Second, he asked God to **establish** them **in every good word and work**. This prayer for *comfort and continued testimony and work for Jesus* is fitting in light of the special needs of believers under pressure.

i. This is a prayer full of useful and important suggestions:

- Jesus is ours.
- God is our Father.
- God has loved us.
- God has given us much.
- We have **everlasting consolation**.
- It is all through grace.

ii. **And establish you**: "I believe in an established Church, not established by acts of Parliament but stablished by the purpose and by the presence of God in the midst of it." (Spurgeon)

c. **In every good word and work**: There is some textual evidence that Paul originally put the order as *every good work and word*. Though this is a small difference, Charles Spurgeon saw an important distinction in the order.

i. "Some Christian people think that 'word' should be everything and work nothing, but the Scriptures are not of their mind. These professors speak a great deal about what they will do, talk a great deal about what other people ought to do, and a great deal more about what others fail to do; and so they go on with word, word, word, and nothing else but word. They do not get as far as 'work,' but the apostle put work first in this case." (Spurgeon)

•

2 Thessalonians 3 - Guidance for Church Life

A. Prayer requested and given.

1. (1-2) Paul's prayer request.

Finally, brethren, pray for us, that the word of the Lord may run *swiftly* and be glorified, just as *it is* with you, and that we may be delivered from unreasonable and wicked men; for not all have faith.

a. **Finally, brethren, pray for us**: Paul constantly asked other Christians to pray for him (Romans 15:30, 2 Corinthians 1:11, Ephesians 6:18-19, Philippians 1:19, Colossians 4:3, 1 Thessalonians 5:25, and Philemon 1:22). Paul knew that the success of his ministry in some measure depended on the prayers of God's people.

i. "You cannot tell how much God's servants are helped by the prayers of his people. The strongest man in Israel will be the better for the prayers of the weakest saint in Zion." (Spurgeon)

b. **That the word of the Lord may run swiftly and be glorified**: Paul's great concern - what he first asked the Thessalonian Christians to pray for - was that God's Word be **free** to do its work among others, even as it had among the Thessalonians (**just as it is with you**).

i. Paul asked for prayer so that the Word can **run** freely, without any hindrance. Paul's prayer request makes us wonder how often the work of God's Word is hindered by our prayerlessness.

ii. God *has* promised that His Word would be free and perform its work: *It shall not return to Me void, but it shall accomplish what I please, and prosper in the thing for which I sent it* (Isaiah 55:11). But as with many of God's promises, we are expected to take this promise in faith, and in prayer, to ask God to perform the promise for His glory.

c. **That we may be delivered from unreasonable and wicked men**: These were those who wanted to hinder the work of the gospel. Paul wanted God to either deliver him from such men, or change them into reasonable and godly men.

2. (3-5) Paul's confidence in the Lord and prayer for the Thessalonians.

But the Lord is faithful, who will establish you and guard *you* from the evil one. And we have confidence in the Lord concerning you, both that you do and will do the things we command you. Now may the Lord direct your hearts into the love of God and into the patience of Christ.

a. **But the Lord is faithful**: Even if not *all* men *have faith,* the **Lord is faithful.** This was the basis of Paul's confidence in God's ability to **establish** and **guard** us from the **evil one**.

i. God promised to keep Satan on a leash. He will not allow any temptation to become too great for us (1 Corinthians 10:13), and will not allow Satan to do whatever he wants with us (Luke 22:31-32).

b. **And we have confidence in the Lord**: Paul was also confident (**in the Lord**) regarding the Thessalonians themselves, that they would follow through and be obedient to God's Word (**that you do and will do the things we command you**). This shows that God's work of establishing and guarding us is done, in part, through His appeal to our will in obeying His Word.

i. God doesn't just pour spiritual maturity and stability into us. He works it in us through our cooperation with His will.

c. **Now may the Lord direct your hearts**: Towards this end, Paul wisely prayed for both **love** and **patience** (endurance) for the Thessalonian Christians. These were two qualities essential for the kind of spiritual stability and strength the Thessalonians needed.

B. Instructions for the strength and purity of the church.

1. (6) The command to withdraw from the disorderly.

But we command you, brethren, in the name of our Lord Jesus Christ, that you withdraw from every brother who walks disorderly and not according to the tradition which he received from us.

a. **But we command you**: The strength of this statement is plain. It was not only a **command**, but it was also made **in the name of our Lord Jesus Christ**.

b. **That you withdraw from every brother who walks disorderly**: Paul defined the **disorderly** as those who did not walk **according to the tradition** (the pattern of teaching and living) Paul and the apostles gave to them.

i. Churches should never withdraw from someone because he fails to conform to *man's* traditions or teachings. The only standard to uphold is *apostolic* tradition and teaching.

ii. "The present tense of the verb *walks* denotes that it is a deliberate course of action. Their disorderly conduct is not an occasional lapse but a persistent practice." (Hiebert)

c. **Withdraw from every brother**: Paul had already told the Thessalonians to *warn the unruly* (1 Thessalonians 5:14). Apparently, the problem still remained in some measure, so he told them to now discipline the *unruly* ones in question.

i. The purpose in withdrawing from these disobedient was not so much punishment, but more so simply to deny these disobedient ones the aid and comfort of the fellowship of the body of Christ until they repented. It put them out of the church into the "domain" of Satan (the world), in hope that they might miss the fellowship of the church so much they would repent of their disobedience.

ii. Paul echoed the same idea in 1 Corinthians 5:4-5. The purpose was to bring about repentance and salvation in the disobedient ones, not to condemn or damn them.

iii. In an indirect way, Paul showed that his vision for the church was that it should be such a place of love and comfort that one would genuinely feel sad and sorry to be excluded from the church. Churches today should also fit that description.

2. (7-9) Paul describes the life displayed by the apostolic tradition.

For you yourselves know how you ought to follow us, for we were not disorderly among you; nor did we eat anyone's bread free of charge, but worked with labor and toil night and day, that we might not be a burden to any of you, not because we do not have authority, but to make ourselves an example of how you should follow us.

a. **For you yourselves know how you ought to follow us**: Paul was an excellent example among the Thessalonians, in that he worked hard to support his own needs. This wasn't because apostles like Paul didn't have the right to request support. Instead, it was because he wanted to set a good example of hard work and prove false any accusation that he preached the Gospel for personal gain.

b. **To make ourselves an example of how you should follow us**: Therefore, the Thessalonians should follow Paul in his example of both hard work and willingness to sacrifice for the furtherance and integrity of the Gospel.

3. (10) Paul describes the teaching presented by the apostolic tradition.

For even when we were with you, we commanded you this: If anyone will not work, neither shall he eat.

a. **If anyone will not work, neither shall he eat**: Simply put, Paul says that if anyone **will not work** (instead of *can not work*), **neither shall he eat**. God's plan is to provide for our needs through our work.

b. **Neither shall he eat**: Since God is able to provide through our needs in any manner imaginable, it means something that He has chosen (for the most part) to meet our needs through work. This is part of God's character, because He is a busy God and always at work.

4. (11-13) Paul applies the apostolic tradition to the situation among the Thessalonians.

For we hear that there are some who walk among you in a disorderly manner, not working at all, but are busybodies. Now those who are such we command and exhort through our Lord Jesus Christ that they work in quietness and eat their own bread. But *as for* you, brethren, do not grow weary *in* doing good.

a. **There are some who walk among you in a disorderly manner**: The idleness of some had become a source of sin. It was not only because of the work that they *didn't do*, but also because of the harm they *did do* with their idle time (**but are busybodies**).

i. There is a play on words between the ancient Greek phrasing in the lines **not working at all** and **but are busybodies**. The idea is something like "busybodies who do no business."

ii. Perhaps these **busybodies** thought that if Jesus was coming soon, it made no sense to work. It would then be easy for them to intrude into the lives of others and take advantage of Christian generosity.

iii. "It is the inactive drones whom Paul is berating – those who live by the sweat of others while they themselves do nothing for the common good to help the human race, such as our monks and priests who acquire ample dimensions by their inactivity." (Calvin)

b. **Now those who are such we command**: With authority, **through our Lord Jesus**, Paul commanded these **busybodies** to **work**, to get out of the business of others (**in quietness**) and to provide for their own needs (**eat their own bread**) instead of expecting other Christians to provide for them.

i. The early church did provide for the truly needy among them, but only after being certain that they were truly needy and after putting them to work for the church (1 Timothy 5:3-16).

ii. "Paul forbids the Thessalonians to encourage their laziness by indulging it, and teaches that it is those who proved themselves with the necessities of life by honourable and useful work that lead a life of holiness." (Calvin)

c. **Do not grow weary in doing good**: This was a proper encouragement for those who were working as they should. Few things are more wearying than seeing others take advantage of Christian generosity. But we should never let the manipulations of some discourage us from doing good to the truly needy.

i. The older King James Version has this, *be not weary in well doing*. There is plenty of *well-wishing* in the world. *Well-resolving, well-suggesting*, and *well-criticizing* are also found in plenty. Many people are good at *well-talking*, but there is not enough of simple *well doing*.

ii. "But well doing consists in taking down the shutters and selling your goods; tucking up your shirt sleeves and doing a good day's work; sweeping the carpets and dusting the chairs, if you happen to be a domestic servant. Well doing is attending to the duties that arise out of our relationships in life – attending carefully to them, and seeing that in nothing we are eye-servers and men-pleasers, but in everything are seeking to serve God." (Spurgeon)

iii. There are many excuses one might make to allowing weariness in **doing good**, but they should all be rejected.

- "It takes so much effort to keep doing good" – but you will extend effort towards the things of the world.

- "It takes so much self-denial to keep doing good" – but it is worth it when we consider the reward.

- "It just brings me persecution to do good" – but your persecutions are nothing compared to that which others have suffered.

- "People don't respond and there are little results when I do good" – but remember how slow you were to respond to Jesus Christ.

- "It doesn't earn much gratitude when I do good" – but God sends many blessings even to those who do not thank or appreciate Him.

5. (14-15) More on how to deal with the disobedient.

And if anyone does not obey our word in this epistle, note that person and do not keep company with him, that he may be ashamed. Yet do not count *him* as an enemy, but admonish *him* as a brother.

a. **And if anyone does not obey our word in this epistle**: Here, Paul finished the thought introduced at 2 Thessalonians 3:6. He here elaborates on what it means to *withdraw* from a brother as mentioned previously.

b. **Note that person and do not keep company with him**: To *withdraw* means to **note that person**, and to **not keep company with him**, with the purpose of causing him to **be ashamed**. Yet, the purpose is not to make him an **enemy** of the church, but through the severity of the withdrawal from fellowship, to warn and **admonish** him as an erring **brother**.

i. "The intention of excommunication is not to drive men from the Lord's flock, but rather to bring them back again when they have wandered and gone astray... Excommunication is to be distinguished from anathema." (Calvin)

6. (16-18) Conclusion to the letter.

Now may the Lord of peace Himself give you peace always in every way. The Lord *be* with you all. The salutation of Paul with my own hand, which is a sign in every epistle; so I write. The grace of our Lord Jesus Christ *be* with you all. Amen.

a. **Now may the Lord of peace**: Paul's blessing of **peace** (**always in every way**) was appropriate for this church experiencing both persecution and tribulation. It is the presence of the **Lord of peace** that will grant them this peace.

i. "I want to call particular attention to the apostle's words in this place. He does not say 'May the Lord of peace send his angel to give you peace.' It were a great mercy if he did, and we might be as glad as Jacob was at Mahanaim, when the angels of God met him. He does not even say, 'May the Lord of peace send his minister to give you peace.' If he did we might be as happy as Abraham when Melchizedec refreshed him with bread and wine. He does not even say, 'May the Lord of peace at the communion table, or in reading the word, or in prayer, or in some other sacred exercise give you peace.' In all these we might well be as refreshed ... but he says 'the Lord of peace himself give you peace,' as if he alone in his own person could give peace, and as if his presence were the sole means of such a divine peace as he desires." (Spurgeon)

b. **The salutation of Paul with my own hand**: As was his custom, Paul himself wrote the final words of the epistle with his own hand. This was both a personal demonstration of affection, and proof that the letter was authentic (**a sign in every epistle**).

c. **The grace of our Lord Jesus Christ be with you all**: For Paul, God's **grace** was the beginning and the end of the Christian life. It was appropriate that this letter - and most - of his letters began and ended with a mention of **grace**.

> i. "There is the addition of one little word in this final benediction as compared with its form in the first Epistle. It is the word '*all.*' Thus the apostle takes those whom he had been rebuking and correcting, and so reveals the greatness of his heart and his love." (Morgan)

> ii. "Thus he poureth out his affection, by prayer upon prayer for them. A sweet closing up!" (Trapp)

Bibliography - 1-2 Thessalonians

Alford, Henry "The First Epistle of Paul the Apostle to the Thessalonians," *The New Testament for English Readers, Volume II, Part I* (London: Rivingtons, 1869)

Barclay, William *The Letters to the Philippians, Colossians, and Thessalonians* (Philadelphia: Westminster Press, 1975)

Calvin, John *The Epistles of Paul to the Thessalonians*, translated by R. Mackenzie (Grand Rapids, Michigan: Eerdmans, 1960)

Clarke, Adam *The New Testament with A Commentary and Critical Notes, Volume II* (New York: Eaton & Mains, 1831)

Hiebert, D. Edmond *The Thessalonians Epistles: A Call to Readiness* (Chicago: Moody Press, 1971)

Meyer, F.B. *Our Daily Homily* (Westwood, New Jersey: Revell, 1966)

Moffatt, James D.D. "The First and Second Epistles to the Thessalonians," *The Expositor's Greek New Testament, Volume IV* (London: Hodder and Stoughton, date uncertain)

Morgan, G. Campbell *An Exposition of the Whole Bible* (Old Tappan, New Jersey: Revell, 1959)

Morgan, G. Campbell *Searchlights from the Word* (New York, Revell: 1936)

Morris, Leon *The First and Second Epistles to the Thessalonians* (Grand Rapids, Michigan: Eerdmans, 1959)

Poole, Matthew *A Commentary on the Holy Bible, Volume III: Matthew-Revelation* (London: Banner of Truth Trust, 1969, first published in 1685)

Spurgeon, Charles Haddon *The New Park Street Pulpit, Volumes 1-6* and *The Metropolitan Tabernacle Pulpit, Volumes 7-63* (Pasadena, Texas: Pilgrim Publications, 1990)

Thomas, Robert L. "1 Thessalonians," *The Expositor's Bible Commentary, Volume 11* (Grand Rapids, Michigan: Zondervan, 1978)

Trapp, John *A Commentary on the Old and New Testaments, Volume Five* (Eureka, California: Tanski Publications, 1997)

As the years pass I love the work of studying, learning, and teaching the Bible more than ever. I'm so grateful that God is faithful to meet me in His Word.

Thanks once again to Martina Patrick for her proofreading help. She is always patient with my work, even when I make the same mistakes over and over through a manuscript.

Thanks to Brian Procedo for the cover design and all the graphics work.

Most especially, thanks to my wife Inga-Lill. She is my loved and valued partner in life and in service to God and His people.

David Guzik

David Guzik's Bible commentary is regularly used and trusted by many thousands who want to know the Bible better. Pastors, teachers, class leaders, and everyday Christians find his commentary helpful for their own understanding and explanation of the Bible. David and his wife Inga-Lill live in Santa Barbara, California.

You can email David at
david@enduringword.com

For more resources by David Guzik,
go to www.enduringword.com

CPSIA information can be obtained
at www.ICGtesting.com
Printed in the USA
BVHW031152220122
626773BV00005B/468